Resilience and Psychological First Aid

For Community Emergency Responders

Nick Arnett

https://nickarnett.net

Facebook: StressIntoStrengthBook

YouTube: Stress Into Strength

Twitter: NickArnett

Eventbrite (training): https://bit.ly/ResilWebinar

Email: mailto:nick.arnett+rfpabook@gmail.com

This book is dedicated to those who make their community better prepared for emergencies and disasters.

Contents

Preface

In mid-March of 2020, just after Santa Clara County, where I live, issued the nation's first shelter-in-place public health order, a friend at one of our Community Emergency Response Teams (CERT), aware that I was teaching resilience classes for public safety, asked me if I'd do the same for them. The next day, I was in a video conference teaching the material that has led to this book. Soon, I published a short book, *Resilience During the Pandemic*, using material I had developed for a much larger one that HarperCollins Leadership will publish in 2021 *(Stress Into Strength: Resilience Routines for Warriors, Wimps, and Everyone in Between)*.

In June and July, I began offering the webinar to people interested in CERT. The response has been amazing. Thousands of people have participated and the compliments could give me a big head, along with the incredibly positive reviews of *Resilience During the Pandemic.*

Clearly, people are feeling the need for this material. I'm grateful for the gifts of writing and speaking; never in my life has my work felt more like a gift than during this time. I hope this information and whatever wisdom I am offering will help you to serve your family, friends, community, and yourself during these challenging and difficult times.

One: Resilience

Much of this book is about how **you** can become more resilient, to bounce back faster from adversity. The reason for focusing on you before talking about helping others will become clear as you read. But here's a hint: You can't give away what you don't have. Also, helping others helps you. That is how humans are wired.

Why teach or learn resilience? That is a reasonable question, especially since science long regarded resilience as something you had to be born with. But in recent years, as technology has allowed researchers to peek inside our brains, it has become clear that we can rewire them. In other words, just as we are not stuck with the bodies we are born with, we can strengthen and

> **Neuroplasticity**
> The brain's ability to form and reorganize synaptic connections, especially in response to learning, experience, or following injury.

transform our minds. We are also learning that resilience is about more than just mindset. The "second brain" in your gut, your muscles, and other parts of your physiology, are also involved.

We know that teaching resilience is worthwhile because we can see that it works. Psychological studies show that when people learn and practice healthy rhythms of physical, social, and spiritual[1] exercise and renewal, their stress reactions become less extreme and fade away faster. Your response to life's ups and downs becomes more flexible.

Contrary to what you often hear, stress is not bad for you. Although extreme or chronic stress can hurt you, moderate and intermittent stress makes you *stronger*

---

[1] By "spiritual" I mean values, meaning, and purpose to life that rises above self-interest. Religion can be a source of these, but not the only one.

when you combine it with the right kinds and amounts of renewal activation, as I will describe. Unfortunately, when people believe in "toxic stress," *that very belief* makes their stress reaction stick, which certainly is harmful.

A few years ago, a study by University of Wisconsin researchers showed this persuasively. This was no small study. The scientists looked at 30,000 U.S. adults who had filled out a health and stress survey eight years earlier, to see who had lived and who had died. As you might expect, those who reported high stress were the quickest to die – but only if they also believed that stress

> **The Wisconsin Study**
> Keller, Abiola, Kristin Litzelman, Lauren E. Wisk, Torsheika Maddox, Erika Rose Cheng, Paul D. Creswell, and Whitney P. Witt. 2012. "Does the Perception That Stress Affects Health Matter? The Association with Health and Mortality." Health Psychology 31 (5): 677–84.

harms health. Their startling discovery was that those

who reported the highest stress but did not believe it is unhealthy, *lived the longest.*

Stress reactions are your friend when they help you seize opportunities, rise to challenges, and cope with threats. They give you short-term energy, stamina, and focus. It is true that stress will wear you down in the long run – if, and this is the *big if,* you don't regularly activate renewal appropriate to the stress you experience.

You are not a mere machine. Unlike machines, when living things get the right kinds and amounts of stress and renewal, at the right intervals, they grow stronger. In other words, healthy, resilient people become that way through regular rhythms of stress and renewal: *resilience routines.*

A year before the Covid-19 pandemic, as I recognized how technology and social change have led to disconnection from sources of renewal, I was telling students "More than ever, we need to know how to be more resilient."

Pandemic stress has accelerated our disconnection, so we need to be more intentional about renewal than ever. To regain and build our strength as individuals, communities, and as a species, we need to rebuild courageous, caring, committed connections with the physical world, each other, and trustworthy sources of meaning and values.

Summary

Resilience means bouncing back faster from adversity. Helping others be more resilient can also help you. Although stress that is excessive or chronic can hurt you, moderate stress combined with appropriate renewal – the right kinds, amounts, and rhythms – makes you stronger. "Toxic stress" is a myth; *fear of stress* is toxic, not ordinary stress, which will not wear you down if you also experience appropriate renewal. In an increasingly disconnected culture, we can turn stress into strength through courageous, caring, committed connections – physical, social, and spiritual.

9

Two: Dimensions of Stress and Renewal

Hans Selye, the researcher who first applied the word "stress" to humans in the 1950s, realized that he needed to come up with a better word to describe *sources* of stress. He coined the word "stressor" to avoid the confusion of using the word "stress" to mean both the source and the reaction. Stress and stressors are physical, social, and spiritual.

- Physical stressors can be bodily conditions such as fatigue, cold, sickness, injury, heat, dehydration, and hunger. Debt, bankruptcy, homelessness, lacking tools or skills, and other difficulties involving the material world are also physical stressors.
- Social stressors, which affect us mentally and emotionally, include feeling vulnerable, embarrassed,

unappreciated, lonely, criticized, isolated, or abandoned. Guilt and shame are potent social stressors with spiritual aspects.

- **Spiritual stressors** show up when life seems meaningless, aimless, or out of control. Betrayal, helplessness, unpredictability, and lack of control are spiritual stressors.

Without renewal, stress becomes cumulative. It is like dropping rocks into a backpack that becomes heavier and heavier, so slowly that you might not even notice, until one day you realize you are carrying an immense weight. We all need opportunities to "empty the backpack." Emergencies and disasters can add a lot of "weight," so it isn't unusual for a crisis to make people notice how much they are carrying or to react out of proportion to the event.

When you feel stress about something, remember that it is *because you care*. We don't feel stress about things we don't care about!

And giving care in a spirit of generosity – to people, pets, plants, and more – is a way to become more resilient.

Healthy rhythms of physical stress and renewal strengthen us for *doing, using, and owning things.* Your body, tools, and "muscle memory" skills give you power over and the need to commit giving and receiving material care.

About 120 years ago, a scientist named Walter B. Cannon came up with a now-familiar phrase to describe our physical stress reaction: *fight or flight.* You probably have heard of that one, but far fewer people know Cannon's phrase describing physical renewal: *rest and digest.*

Healthy rhythms of social stress and renewal strengthen our *thinking and feeling.* They arise from interacting with people, enhancing our ability to regulate emotions and think clearly. You grow your ability to cooperate and compete with others – or just play with and enjoy them!

13

Our response to social stress is to *defend and distance* ourselves from others. We activate social renewal when we *tend and befriend,* which was labeled a stress response primarily seen in females when it was first identified twenty-five years ago.

Despite the original researchers' suggestion that *tend and befriend* is a stress response, it clearly drives renewal. Oxytocin triggers repair of harm done by stress hormones, such as heart muscle damaged by adrenaline. Under stress, relationships – friendships, marriages, business partnership – break down, but oxytocin urges us to repair social connections. It enhances our ability to recognize facial

> The main hormone associated with *tend and befriend* is oxytocin, sometimes called the "cuddle hormone," (some kinds of touch increases it). It has even been called a "moral hormone" because it is associated with honesty and altruism (but that appears to be true only among allies).

expressions, to distinguish friend from foe, and to bond with others.

Healthy rhythms of spiritual stress and renewal strengthen our priorities, perspective, and purpose as we change our minds about what is truly important.

Our spiritual stress reaction is to become more *selfish and survivalist*. In a crisis, we are more apt to take ethical shortcuts, losing sight of values that give life meaning beyond self-interest. To activate spiritual renewal, we need to *pause and plan*, to restore our perspective, regain the bigger picture of what life means beyond mere endurance.

Summary

Stressors – sources of stress – can be physical, social, and spiritual. Stress becomes cumulative if you don't experience renewal appropriate to the type and intensity of the stress. In crisis, people often become aware of how much stress was already in the "backpack." We only stress about things we care about – and caring creates resilience.

Stress combined with renewal builds strength when you get the right kinds and amounts in the right rhythms.

	Stress Response	Recovery Response	Strength
Physical	Fight or Flight	Rest and Digest	Doing
Social	Defend or Distance	Tend and Befriend	Thinking, Feeling
Spiritual	Selfish or Survivalist	Pause and Plan	Purpose, Priorities

Three: Rhythms of Stress and Renewal

Think of building your resilience, whether physical, mental, or spiritual, the same way you would build physical strength through weight training – regular intervals of stress followed by renewal.

If you have had CERT or other public safety training, you know that your own safety comes first. You also need to look out for the safety of those you might assist. In psychological first aid, you'll learn about setting up physical, emotional, and spiritual safety. In weight training, safety means using equipment properly and avoiding over-doing it.

- Be courageous. Choose an activity that is beyond your comfort zone – but only a bit. In weight training, this means not overdoing the size or

movement. In social support settings, it means lim-
iting self-disclosure – there is no need to confess all
of your shortcomings at once, especially if you are
with people you don't know well enough to fully
trust to keep confidentiality. Getting out of your
comfort zone spiritually means allowing yourself
into situations that tempt you – but not too much –
to violate your own values and ethics.

- **Be committed.** Notice what is going on with yourself. Stress blinds us to the bigger picture. Observe
yourself as objectively as you can. Use a technique
psychologists call "self-distancing" – observe yourself – to help pay attention to your technique, reactions, and long-term progress. Keeping records
helps you keep the big picture in view.

- Rhythm is important. Just like waiting the right
time between physical sets and workouts, you need
renewal from the time you "sprint" through social
or spiritual stress. You get no benefit from stress

without renewal. Find the right cadence of rest, nu-
trition, social support, and "doing nothing" time between stressful times.

- **Be caring.** Remember why you are "exercising" and
the good it's doing. Start small and when you don't
keep to your desired schedule, just start over.

To repeat, none of this is meant to imply that stress is
never harmful. Again, it is like weightlifting.

- If you lift too much weight, that can hurt you. Get
out of your comfort zone, but not too far.
- If you lift weights too often – not pausing between
sets or not taking time off from lifting – you will
wear yourself down and fail to grow stronger.
- If you fail to *rest and digest* properly – get enough
sleep and protein, your muscles will not repair
properly, nor will they grow.

- If you lift other people's weights for them – code-pendence – you'll both suffer. You will be lifting too much; they will be lifting too little.

I've used the phrase "appropriate renewal" because too much renewal is as bad as too much stress. Excessive physical renewal activation might be resting too much (avoiding the stress of exercise), eating too much, or abusing painkillers. Too much social renewal activation looks like socializing too much, worrying too much about pleasing others, or avoiding conflict. Excessive spiritual renewal activation can result in becoming rigid in your beliefs, thinking you are always right; or using anger and aggression to get your way.

Your Stress Autopilot

Your stress reactions are automatic – you have little or no *logical* control over them. The part of your brain that monitors for opportunities, challenges, and threats (amygdala and limbic system), is like an autopilot that tries to take over when it senses a pattern where fast re-actions, extra energy, stamina, and focus might be helpful. We are wired with some of those patterns, such as an automatic fear of heights. We learn others through experience.

The more stress you experience without appropriate renewal, the more you tend be on autopilot. It "yells louder" than the part of your brain that is logical (your pre-frontal cortex). In other words, these two parts of your brain compete to be in charge. The stronger your stress reaction, the more your stress autopilot is in charge.

You cannot reason with your stress autopilot; it only learns from experience. The kinds of experiences that help it learn to calm down quickly after stress and activate re-newal are safety, companionship, and predictability. We get those from courageous, caring, committed connections.

Building new habits – resilience routines – is simple, but not easy. Don't confuse the rewards with the journey. Resilient people have more motivation and greater self-discipline. However, these are the *results* of resilience routines, not the way you get there.

Let these simple instructions be your mantra for building new habits (or ending bad ones):

Start small. Start over.

Be gentle with yourself – give yourself unlimited permission to fail and begin again.

Although building resilience means developing habits such as a healthy diet and exercise, let go of the "shoulds" that we often tell ourselves. Stop telling yourself you *should* or *ought to* eat better or work out more. Instead, do what psychologists call "positive reframing." Tell yourself,

"I'm going to skip those potato chips because I'll be healthier without them." "I'm exercising because it will make me stronger."

The problem with the "shoulds" is that when you have strong beliefs and fail – because nobody is perfect – that's a trigger for guilt or worse, shame, both of which are potent stress autopilot activators. The more activated your stress autopilot is, the *less* self-discipline, motivation, willpower, and impulse control you have.

Because your stress autopilot and "executive center" compete for dominance, guilt and shame can drown out your executive function. Can you see the vicious cycle that results? You set an impossible standard with a "should," inevitably fall short, elevating your stress response, making it even *harder* to achieve your goal. Meanwhile, your chronically activated stress reaction wears you down.

The antidote to the "shoulds" is *self-compassion.* Be as kind and gentle with yourself as you would be with a friend going through the same thing. Strive for progress, not perfection, and keep in mind that progress is never a straight line. Maintain a long-term perspective. *Courageous, committed, caring connection* applies to yourself, too.

Never mistake short-term failure for a character flaw.

The next three chapters will dive deeper into the physical, social/mental, and spiritual dimensions of resilience.

Summary

Building resilience requires regular intervals of stress and renewal. The steps include safety, getting out of your comfort zone, self-distancing and record-keeping, finding the right cadence, thinking positively, starting small and starting over. Stress can harm you – too much, too often, insufficient renewal, or taking on too much of others' stress. Too much renewal activation – such as resting, eating, socializing, avoiding conflict, rigid beliefs – is also bad for you. Your stress autopilot is pre-wired and learns through experience. It gives you fast reactions, energy, stamina, and focus. It competes with your brain's logical center to be charge. Safety, companionship, and predictability calm the autopilot. When it is active, you have less self-discipline, willpower, and impulse control, so you cannot rely on them to get started. Instead, start small, start over, and be gentle with yourself, practicing self-compassion. Progress, not perfection!

Four: Building Physical Resilience

Physical skills, well-being, and resilience are the result of healthy rhythms of activating your "fight or flight" and "rest and digest" stress and renewal reactions. This develops physical strength, for doing, caring for, and using things.

You are undoubtedly familiar with one way to trigger your physical "fight or flight" reaction – exercise! If you walk, run, lift weights, or any other kind, your stress reaction raises your heart rate, speeds your breathing, and drives other changes that give you energy and focus to perform. When you *choose* physical stress that is a bit outside of your comfort zone, your autopilot activates at a moderate level and will quiet faster than when stress is out of your control. In other words, exercise keeps the door open for renewal, avoiding the perils of chronic stress. You know when you are experiencing healthy physical stress when it tires you out without causing injury or excess fatigue.

Building "muscle memory," such as learning to drive or ride a bicycle (which mainly takes place in your brain, not muscles), also activates your stress reactions. Moderate increases in stress hormones help you to learn, practice, and remember a skill.

Using and managing things also triggers a physical stress reaction. Homes need to be cleaned, cars need maintenance, food has to be prepared, and so forth. Like workouts, this kind of stress is helpful when you don't have too little or too much. Too few possessions and your stress autopilot will react to the lack of safety and security; too much and you may feel burdened and distracted by the overload.

Your physical stress only becomes strength if you also "rest and digest." Nourishment and sleep are essential, but before we get to those, there are some shortcuts, mind/body practices that directly awaken and strengthen your renewal responses.

Where you give your attention is important. The exercises that follow are examples to help you relax and build *interoception,* a fancy word for attending to what is going on with your mind and body.

Breathing and Heart Rate Variability (HRV)

Controlled breathing is a shortcut for awakening your vagus nerve, the biggest nerve in your body, which connects your gut to your brain. The more active it is ("vagal tone"), the more resilient you are, physically and mentally. It is central to your parasympathetic nervous system, which prompts *rest and digest.* When you exhale, your heart slows down slightly. It speeds up again as you inhale. That's called heart rate variability, or HRV. The higher your HRV, the more resilient you are, physically and psychologically.

Thanks to technology, you can even monitor and improve your HRV through biofeedback. If this appeals to you, get the kind of heart monitor that goes around your chest (most of the wrist ones aren't accurate enough) that talks to an app on your smart phone. Apps coach you to control your breathing and show your HRV. Over time, you can increase it, training your mind and body to activate renewal faster after stressful events, making you more resilient.

You don't need to invest in technology to gain these benefits. All healthy rhythms of stress and renewal practiced regularly do the same. The following "shortcuts" can help you bounce back faster from stress and increasingly turn it into strength.

Belly breathing

This is also called diaphragmatic breathing, because it trains you to breathe deeply, rather than the shallow way we breathe under stress.

- Comfortably lie on your back in bed, or on the floor, with a pillow under your head and knees. Or you can sit in a chair with your shoulders, head, and neck supported against its back.
- Breathe in through your nose; let your chest fill with air.
- Breathe out through your nose.
- Place one hand on your belly and the other on your chest.
- As you breathe in, feel your belly rise; as you breathe out, feel your belly lower. The hand on your belly should move more than the one on your chest.

- Take at least three more full, deep breaths. Breathe fully into your belly, as it rises and falls with your breath.
- Notice how you feel when you are done.

4-7-8 Breathing

You can do this sitting or lying down.

- To start, put one hand on your belly and the other on your chest, as in belly breathing.
- Take a deep, slow breath from your belly, and silently count to four, as you breathe in.
- Hold your breath and silently count from one to seven.
- Breathe out completely, as you silently count from one to eight. Try to get all of the air out of your lungs by the time you reach eight.
- Repeat three to seven times, or until you feel calm.
- Notice how you feel when you are done.

Roll Breathing

This helps you to learn to use your entire lungs while focusing on your breathing rhythm. You can do it in any position. While you are learning, it is best to lie on your back with your knees bent.

- Put your left hand on your belly and your right hand on your chest. Notice how your hands move as you breathe in and out.
- Practice filling your lower lungs by breathing so that your left hand (on your belly) goes up when you inhale and your right hand (on your chest) stays still. Breathe in through your nose and out through your mouth. Do this eight to ten times.
- Add the second step: inhale first into your lower lungs as before, and then continue inhaling into your upper chest. Breathe slowly and regularly. Your right hand will rise and your left hand will drop a little as your belly falls.

- As you exhale slowly through your mouth, make a quiet, whooshing sound as your left hand and then your right hand drop. As you exhale, feel tension leaving your body.
- Practice breathing this way for three to five minutes. Notice that your belly and chest movements rise and fall like the movement of rolling waves.
- Notice how you feel at the end of the exercise.

Practice roll breathing daily for several weeks. You can use it as an instant relaxation tool.

5-4-3-2-1 Grounding

Taking a moment to *notice* things around you can turn down anxiety. "Grounding" helps you connect to the physical world. This method works for many people, including children.

- Name five things that you can see in the room with you;
- Name four things that you can feel right now;
- Name three things that you can hear right now;
- Name two things that you can smell right now (or two things that you like the smell of);
- Name one good thing about yourself.

Tapping is another form of grounding; "Butterfly Hug" tapping is easy (and easy to teach to children):

- Fold your arms over your chest, so that you can tap between your collarbone and shoulder…
- Let your mind drift, while you slowly tap yourself alternatively with each hand – do this for thirty seconds.

Most people find this relaxing. If you don't want what you're doing to be so obvious, you can do something similar by tapping your thighs alternatively – it works a little better if you cross your arms.

Progressive Muscle Relaxation (PMR)

To do PMR, you tighten one muscle group at a time, followed by relaxation. You can do it lying down or seated, but it works best if you choose a location free of distractions.

Warming up with one of the deep breathing techniques can help to prepare you.

- While inhaling, contract a muscle group for five to ten seconds, then exhale and release the tension.
- Give yourself ten to twenty seconds to relax, then move on to the next muscle group...
- While releasing the tension, try to focus on the changes you feel when the muscle group relaxes –

36

imagery may be helpful, such as picturing stressful feelings flowing out of your body as you relax.

- Gradually work your way up your body, contracting and relaxing muscle groups.

Muscle groups for PMR:
1. Forehead.
2. Jaw.
3. Neck and shoulders.
4. Arms and hands.
5. Buttocks.
6. Legs.
7. Feet.

Mind/Body Disciplines

Practices such as yoga, Pilates, Tai Chi, and martial arts will also help you build interoception and activate physical renewal. They can be both stressful and relaxing, but making them a habit will help your brain and body respond to stress more flexibly. You will relax and renew faster when the sources of stress are gone.

Bear in mind that our bodies store stress; you may find these practices intimidating and even painful as they turn your attention to what you are physically holding onto. Again, *noticing* is the first step toward letting go. If this topic interests you, try reading Bessel van der Kolk's outstanding book, *The Body Keeps the Score.*

Diet

Some foods nourish your stress response by giving you fast energy. Others feed renewal by providing the building blocks for long-term health and strength. Eating too much fast-energy food – sugars, starches, and other carbohydrates – feeds the inflammatory response that accompanies stress. Inflammation is linked to many physical and mental health issues, from cardiovascular disease to depression.

An anti-inflammatory diet encourages renewal. It includes fruits and vegetables (especially leafy greens), whole grains, plant-based proteins (beans, nuts, etc.) fish high in Omega-3 oils (tuna, salmon, sardines).

Eat inclusively, which means tossing out hard-and-fast rules (which nearly always backfire). You can have your favorite foods if you aim for variety. When you eat, you aren't just feeding yourself, you are also feeding the organisms that live in your gut, which we now realize are vitally important to physical and mental health. The health of your "gut biome," also sometimes called your gut fauna or microbiome, is linked to dozens of illnesses of the body and mind.

Even though we know that the gut biome is critically important, it is not well understood. One thing we know for sure: diversity is essential. Having about a thousand different organisms is healthy, but we know little about the best assortment. Only a few important ones have been identified. Be skeptical of "probiotic supplements" that claim to provide the right kinds. Eat probiotic *foods*, many of which result from fermentation. Yogurt, kefir, apple cider vinegar, sauerkraut, pickles, traditional buttermilk, and certain cheeses are powerful probiotics. And one more food that you might not realize is fermented: chocolate! Dark chocolate is what you want, to avoid the carbs in sweeter kinds. Note that anything pasteurized cannot give you beneficial organisms; they are killed along with the unwanted ones.

In addition to probiotic foods, you need *pre-biotics,* which feed your gut fauna. These often are indigestible carbohydrates, such as fiber. Legumes, beans, peas, oats, apples, berries, garlic, onions, asparagus, and bananas are prebiotic foods.

See why processed foods are bad for you? They provide little or no nourishment for your gut biome. Meanwhile, *you* get too many calories. "Easy" eating is a bad strategy, just as when exercising at the gym.

Avoid foods with trans fats (often found in snacks so that they don't need to be refrigerated), fried foods, soft drinks (a 12-ounce soda has the equivalent of *twenty-five* sugar packets!!), and anything labeled "low fat" or "low carb" (such as diet soft drinks) because those tend to over-stimulate your appetite.

Sleep

Sufficient, quality sleep is vitally important and too many people aren't getting enough. Almost all adults need seven to eight hours of "sleep opportunity" per night. Even if you think you can get by on four or five hours, you probably are wrong. Now that advanced technology allows us to see what happens during sleep, we know that sleep deprivation usually has serious long-term ill effects for people who may think they are getting enough.

Researchers found that people with severe Covid-19 often have low melatonin, the hormone that helps us get to sleep. Poor sleep hampers the immune system, which may be one reason the illness hits some people harder.

Take a look at the top ten causes of death: Every one of them is aggravated by insufficient quality sleep. These illnesses cause a lot of suffering. Get enough deep sleep.

Following a traumatic experience (primary or secondary), getting Rapid Eye Movement (REM) sleep is especially important. During REM sleep, our brains disconnect memories of traumatic events from the accompanying emotions, which allows you to remember without feeling as if it is happening all over again. People who don't get sufficient REM sleep are more susceptible to post-traumatic stress injuries. As a provider of PFA, you can expect to experience secondary trauma and recognize that it is just as real as the trauma experienced by those you assist.

For a few days after a high-stress event, avoid substances that disrupt REM sleep. These include alcohol and anti-anxiety drugs such as "benzos": diazepam (Valium), lorazepam (Ativan), alprazolam (Xanax). Many older sleep medications can also interfere with REM sleep. If you need something to help you sleep – which most sleep experts say should be a last resort – consult your doctor and

ask for something that doesn't interfere with REM sleep. Many newer sleep medications are suitable.

If you have sleep apnea, using your CPAP or other treatment is especially important after trauma.

Even a small amount of alcohol in the hours leading up to sleep can interfere with REM sleep, so it's best to refrain from drinking for a few days. In theory, you could drink in the morning and it would be out of your system by the time you went to sleep, but I'm not about to recommend drinking in the morning!

Here are sleep hygiene guidelines.

- Avoid stimulants close to bedtime.
- Darken your room for sleeping, get natural light during the day.
- Establish a routine that signals your mind and body that it is time to sleep. Take a warm shower, use

aromatherapy, read, or stretch. The breathing exercises and Progressive Muscle Relaxation described earlier can help.

- Don't pressure yourself to sleep – tell yourself, "I'm getting into bed to rest."

- Stick to a regular sleep schedule whenever you can. My friends in public safety laugh at this – we are constantly having to alter our rhythms, but if you don't have to, don't.

> I can watch any episode of *Everyone Loves Raymond* or *The Big Bang Theory* and fall asleep when I'm tired and wired. I don't watch a lot of TV, but I have seen every episode of those shows, more than once.

- The best temperature to fall and stay asleep is 60-67. (One of the things I dread is having to sleep in a hot, bright tent during the day so that I can work a night shift on a wildfire.)

- Your bedroom should be a haven – no TV, phone calls, or business in bed.

- Avoid screens close to bedtime; use color warming software. Even a low level of blue-tinted light interferes with your body's ability to produce melatonin, the hormone that makes you feel sleepy. I have software on my phone, tablets and desktop computer that automatically turns the display more yellow and orange as bedtime approaches.

- After high-stress events, you can become "tired and wired" – exhausted but unable to fall asleep. Perhaps you have experienced struggling with sleepiness while driving home, only to find yourself wide awake when you get in bed. A psychologist realized that driving gives your brain something *familiar* to focus on, which triggers the sleepiness. Try watching a light comedy you've seen several times before. The familiar sights can have the same effect as driving, making you sleepy.

- Do you wake up rested? If you are concerned, keep a sleep diary and talk to your doctor. Remember that good sleep is critical to your physical and mental health.

Napping can be helpful, but only for reducing daytime sleepiness. *Napping does not replace sleep! Nothing replaces sleep.* If you miss sleep, it is gone forever; despite what many people think, you cannot make it up later. If you nap, aim for at least ten minutes and no more than thirty. If you are on a normal nighttime sleeping schedule, don't nap after about 3 pm, to avoid interfering with getting to sleep in the evening. One more surprising thing about napping – it is only helpful if you do it regularly. Nap regularly or do not nap, there apparently is no in-between.

Good sleep makes it easier to eat well. Poor sleep raises levels of cortisol, a stress hormone that releases energy. High cortisol, among other effects, makes you crave carbohydrates. Ask yourself, next time you are yearning for carbs, "Did I get a good night's sleep?"

Sleep deprivation also interferes with the hormones that tell you when you are full or hungry (leptin and ghrelin). Stopping yourself from over-eating inflammatory foods then becomes difficult indeed. Unfortunately, the story gets a bit worse. Excess carbs cause weight gain, which can further disturb your sleep and hormones. Getting out of this pattern is challenging, but as you read earlier, greater "self-discipline" or "willpower" is *not* the solution. Remember, start small and give yourself unlimited permission to fail and start over.

Summary

Rhythms of activating "fight or flight" and "rest and digest" responses build physical strength and dexterity for doing, caring for, and using things. Getting the right amounts and frequency of exercise, skills practice, and caring for things builds strength. Rest, sleep, and nourishment activate renewal, turning physical stress into strength. Controlled breathing, grounding, progressive muscle relaxation, and mind/body disciplines are shortcuts, which also increase heart rate variability. An anti-inflammatory diet encourages renewal. Poor sleep is linked to many serious illnesses and premature death and interferes with diet-related hormone levels. REM sleep is especially important following traumatic experiences, so avoid substances that interfere with it. Practice good sleep hygiene.

Five: Building Mental and Emotional Resilience

Mental and emotional well-being build from your social stress and renewal reactions: "defend and distance" and "tend and befriend." This develops your strength for thinking clearly and regulating emotions.

In order to build mental and emotional strength, you need to choose to experience some social stress, just as building physical strength means choosing the physical stress of exercise. Choosing social stress means risking transparency and vulnerability – with safe people. Think of opening up with trusted companions as "going to the mental/emotional gym."

Our need for social support varies, but we all benefit from being seen, heard, and accepted for who we really are, and when we offer that gift to others. But just as you should not rush into an intense physical exercise regime, don't rush into this. Build trust as you slowly step out of your comfort zone. Healthy social stress is when you choose to be honestly transparent with trustworthy people, despite feeling a bit vulnerable, embarrassed, guilty, or even shame.

Vulnerability

Brené Brown writes wonderful books about our need for belonging and acceptance as we are, rather than trying to "fit in" as someone we are not. Take a look at her short YouTube video, *The Biggest Myth About Vulnerability* – or any of her other talks and writings. Brown's book, *The Gifts of Imperfection,* is a great starting point and will help you understand her more recent teachings.

Brown brilliantly observes that we tend to see vulnerability as courage in others, but weakness in ourselves.

She is right; vulnerability takes courage. However, I'll caution again: *Take your time.* Figure out if you really can trust people before you open up. If their reaction is to try and "fix" or pity you, or even worse, to gossip about what you disclosed, that betrayal will be painful, indeed. The more trauma, guilt, or shame you carry, the harder it can be to trust and open up.

You may have a lot of false starts before you find what works for you. Remember, self-compassion: You have unlimited permission to fail. **Start small, start over.**

Don't be surprised when you feel your "defend and distance" response activating as you open up or others offer challenging feedback. You may find yourself wishing you were elsewhere. It is normal for anger, sadness, even guilt and shame to surface. Just like sweating at the gym, do it anyway! Again, take it slow; there's no need to go far outside of your comfort zone. Although others may be curious, you don't owe

anyone your story, especially if it involves trauma. Talking can be healing, but it needs to be when and where you feel safe. In Psychological First Aid, you will learn how different kinds of *curiosity* are assets or liabilities when offering social support.

You can choose not to take others' observations personally. Remember that self-distancing is powerful medicine. Aim to be an objective observer of yourself. All of us are blind to some aspects of ourselves; only other people can open our eyes. Also remember that sometimes criticism is more about the other person than you – they may be projecting their own flaws.

Tend and Befriend: Caring and Being Cared For

 Tending and befriending activates social renewal by connecting you to others. Your stress autopilot doesn't like isolation; belonging to a trustworthy community reassures it. What could be better than knowing a community has your back? What could be harder than believing that nobody cares?

Don't confuse isolation, which you don't choose or know when will end, with solitude, which you *choose* for a limited time. Introverts particularly gain energy from solitude. In contrast, extraverts tend to gain energy from being around people. Both need social support at times.

Social support is more than just friendship. It can come from family, teachers, mentors, coaches, teams – those whom you can trust to remain in your life, without judging, when you make mistakes or step out of your comfort zones of thinking and feeling. Acceptance doesn't mean approval – it doesn't mean any kind of judgement. It just means staying present. This gift is just as important to give as to receive.

Animals

When I accompany dog teams from organizations such as Hope Animal-Assisted Crisis Response and K9 First Responders, visiting firefighters, other public safety and communities, I think, "I can't believe they are paying me to do this." Dogs are amazingly skilled at picking up what people need, offering support and comfort. They can't fix anything, they can't shed tears – and those are two reasons they are effective companions, calming people under stress.

I have permission to share a dog story from a Cal Fire captain who was a strike team leader on the terrible North Bay fires of October 2017. He was doing paperwork in fire camp, exhausted, when he saw one of our dog teams approaching. "Don't come over here," he thought. He just wanted to finish up and get some precious sleep. But the dog and handler came to him.

"After about a minute of petting the dog, I could feel myself relaxing and I was so glad they stopped by." That's the amazing power of social support, amplified by touching and eye contact, which connect and calm our nervous systems whether from people or pets.

Horses are also incredibly sensitive to our mental state, although different from dogs. Horses are prey animals –much more ready for "flight" than "fight." Unlike a support dog, who will come to you if you are upset, a horse "coach" will stay back until you are truly calm. That helps you notice what is going on within yourself, a self-awareness step toward resilience. Search for "equine therapy" to find organizations near you.

Our "household" includes three dogs and a horse, and Sunny, a Sun conure parrot. She has made cameos in Zoom resilience and PFA trainings, perched on my shoulder and occasionally talking. She flew into our backyard a few years ago and we couldn't find her owners. I would say now she is ours, except that it's the other way around – she is certain we are her staff. I don't think that parrots can read emotions as dogs and horses can, yet they form strong social bonds, and I know that caring for her creates resilience. She has lived up to the warning a friend gave: "Having a conure is like having a four-year-old that never grows up," yet we are quite attached.

Our experience with Sunny has helped me realize why we see news stories about people trying to bring unusual animals onto airplanes or into stores as emotional support companions. Caring for those creatures does make us more resilient. (Don't take that to mean that I endorse the idea of allowing emotional support peacocks, etc., to go everywhere.) Oh, and yes, this means that cats, despite their attitude, can be a source of resilience, too!

Summary

"Defend and distance" combined with "tend and be-friend," our social stress and renewal responses, build strength for thinking clearly and managing emotions. Building and keeping this strength means choosing so-cially stressful vulnerability and accepting others when they do the same. Healing can come from re-writing your story as you share it, but don't rush. Start small and build trust. Be compassionate with yourself as well as others. Don't take feedback personally. Social support includes friendships and other relationships from which you can learn and grow. Dogs, horses, and other animals can be sources of social support; caring for them also builds up your resilience.

Six: Building Spiritual Resilience

Spiritual well-being comes from combining the spiritual stress reaction, *selfish and survivalist* with *pause and plan* renewal. This develops strength for sticking to your values, priorities, and purpose.

"Do the next right thing," one of my mentors used to tell me whenever I asked for advice. It was frustrating, but when we don't take time to stop and think about our priorities and *why* we make

> *No one ever said on their deathbed "I wish I'd spent more time at the office"* – Rabbi Harold Kushner.

our choices, when we don't *pause and plan*, it is hard to do the next right thing.

After a crisis, things that formerly seemed important often diminish in value as we give more attention to the bigger picture. Reminders of our mortality can be especially powerful. You know you are experiencing healthy spiritual stress when you feel temptation without giving into it.

Psychologists have known for a long time that people with strong bigger-than-self values and sense of meaning and purpose are better off. *Selfish and survivalist*, like all stress reactions, can be good for solving short-term problems, but does harm if we stay stuck there. *Pause and plan* helps us turn off "tunnel vision" and return to the big picture, the long-term perspective.

Pause and Plan v. Replay and Rehearse

Contemplative practices, religious or secular, often are exercises in pausing and planning, consciously or not.

They emphasize being in the present moment, helping to quiet your stress autopilot.

Your autopilot will urge you to find or make meaning from past high-stress events. It replays them, especially when the stakes were high, such life and limb or embarrassment (which are not far from each other emotionally!) It will also urge you to rehearse future crises, sending your mind into "possibility thinking" about what might go wrong.

Remind yourself of the positive purposes of autopilot-driven replay and rehearse. I tell myself, "That's my brain earning its paycheck," even though it can be uncomfortable. Those instincts have made humans extraordinary survivors as a species. Still, when we get stuck in stress, it shows up as excess anxiety from the past and worry about the future.

Mindfulness and Contemplation

Mindfulness and similar practices help you accept, let go of, and quiet anxiety and worry, at least temporarily. Mindful meditation is a good example. Mindfulness in general is about learning to stay present, noticing when your mind has drifted away, which is necessary before you can choose to return. Once again, you need to *notice* what's going on before you can change it. People sometimes think they are bad at mindful meditation or similar practices because they notice that their mind keeps drifting off. They're wrong – they are not bad at it, that is the very "mental muscle" that it exercises!

Contemplative practices that help you to *pause and plan* include meditation, prayer, retreats, keeping a journal, or anything else that "unplugs" you from focusing on the short-term so you can regain perspective. Sometimes a slight variation, pause and *play,* can work wonders, too!

Any exercise that helps you to identify your values and priorities is a spiritual renewal activator. Here's one: Take a look at your checkbook and calendar to see where you are investing your time and resources. Are these the priorities you really want?

Do an Internet search for "values list" and you'll get plenty of results that can help you think about what is most important to you. From those, goals can flow. Goals help you stay engaged and motivated, especially when you keep track – but remember, progress, not perfection.

Summary

Selfish and survivalist combined with *pause and plan* grows your spiritual strength and resilience. All of us face temptations to take shortcuts and violate our values; we are all hypocrites sometimes. Those moments can became strength when we allow them to remind us of what is really important. Strong values and sense of purpose correlate to our well-being. Activate *pause and plan* with contemplative and mind/body practices, including mindfulness. Periodically step back and compare your behavior to the values you would like to follow.

Seven: Two Wolves

An old Cherokee is teaching his grandson about life. "A fight is going on inside me," he says to the boy.

"It is a terrible fight, and it is between two wolves. One is bad – he is anger, envy, sorrow, regret, greed, arrogance, self-pity, guilt, resentment, inferiority, lies, false pride, superiority, and ego." He continues, "The other is good – he is joy, peace, love, hope, serenity, humility, kindness, benevolence, empathy, generosity, truth, compassion, and faith. The same fight is going on inside you – and inside every other person, too."

The grandson thinks about it for a minute and then asks his grandfather, "Which wolf will win?"

The old Cherokee replies, "The one you feed."

I love this story and use it every time I teach because it describes the two parts of your autonomic nervous system that drive stress and renewal reactions. Your "bad" wolf isn't so bad sometimes. It helps you seize opportunities, rise to challenges, and overcome threats. That's your "sympathetic" nervous system and drives "fight or flight," "defend and distance," and "selfish and survivalist." It is bad only when it is overactive or gets involved when no longer needed.

The other part, your "parasympathetic" nervous system (which includes the vagus nerve), the "good" wolf, drives renewal: "rest and digest," "tend and befriend," and "pause and plan."

The story works well because you truly must feed your good wolf. You need to be *intentional* about activating renewal. Your "bad" wolf will take what it wants.

Here's the big mistake we make – we imagine that we can starve the bad wolf. That doesn't work and is the problem with teaching "stress reduction." Escaping the sources of stress does not ensure that you are activating renewal. Running away from problems is the "flight" part of *fight or flight.*

"Stress reduction" is largely a myth. For example, parenting is stressful. How do you reduce that stress? "Sorry kid, there are too many of you and we have to let some of you go." Only the dead have no stress at all – but I hope that having read this far, you realize that's okay because we *need* stress along with renewal.

Summary

Feed your good wolf!

(Yes, that's the whole summary.)

Eight: Gratitude and Generosity

Our brains react much more to negatives than to positives. We are quicker to believe negative information without checking to see if it is true, more likely to repeat it, more likely to tell it to more people, say it louder, and use richer vocabulary. One way to counteract our inbred "negative bias" is to practice gratitude for and generosity with what you have – possessions, skills, connections, values, and more. Stress is disconnecting; gratefully and generously giving and receiving reconnects us and shows commitment, which helps quiet the stress autopilot.

Here's an invitation (not a "should!") to begin building habits of generosity and gratitude, which are rocket fuel for resilience. For thirty days, which don't have to be in a row (remember, start small, with unlimited permission to fail and start over; be gentle with yourself):

- Write down three things you are grateful for.
- Write down three things you are looking forward to.
- Do at least one anonymous act of kindness.

These can be small or large. Let someone merge in front of you in traffic; be grateful when another does the same for you. Fund a college scholarship if that is within your means. As usual, getting a bit outside of your comfort zone helps you grow.

Nine: Community Responses to Disaster

Although individual disaster reactions vary and never progress in a straight line, communities typically go through a series of responses.

- Pre-disaster – This is when people become aware that a disaster might happen – storm warnings, a rapidly moving wildland fire, indications of a pandemic and so forth. People respond by feeling fearful and uncertain. They might also feel shock or disbelief.
- Impact – As disaster hits, people's concern focuses on themselves and loved ones.
- Heroic – During the unfolding response, communities often express gratitude and love for the first responders. However, if the response is inadequate

because there aren't enough resources available to cope with the emergency, the opposite can happen – communities turn against responders, especially leadership, if they perceive that "They are not doing their job."

- Honeymoon – After the crisis peaks and rebuilding begins, people draw together enthusiastically proclaiming, "Together, we will overcome!"
- Disillusionment – Disaster recovery takes a long, long time. Progress can be difficult to see. As the limitations sink in, people become frustrated, angry, depressed, and perhaps cynical.
- Reconstruction – One day, long after the incident is over, the "new normal" becomes just "normal."

"Realistic optimism" is a characteristic of resilient people: Firmly wedded to accepting reality as it is while also holding onto hope. During a disaster, it is normal for people to shift between realism and optimism.

Before a disaster, healthy communities, like resilient people, are both realistic and optimistic. They forecast cash flow, look unflinchingly at challenges and crises, honestly assess their own performance. At the same time, they work to make things better, confident that they always can. As communities move through the stages of disaster reactions, notice how they move between realism and optimism.

- Pre-disaster – Realism and optimism are balanced. Watches or warnings are issued; people become uncertain, fearful, shocked, or perhaps disbelieve.
- Impact – The emergency or disaster hits and optimism vanishes. People become completely focused on the bad thing that is happening. Their concerns focus on themselves and loved ones.
- Heroic – As it appears that the "heroes" are making everything better, optimism takes over.

- Honeymoon – As the community pulls together the sense of social bonding and teamwork adds to their optimism. They become unrealistic about how long and difficult recovery is.
- Disillusionment – the unfounded optimism gives way to reality as it becomes clear that weeks, months, or years of recovery will be needed.
- Reconstruction – when the "new normal" is just normal, optimism and realism are in balance again.

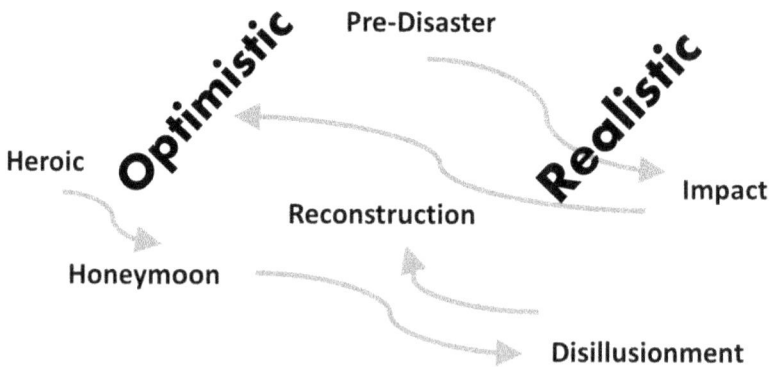

Psychological first aid throughout these phases calls on you to encourage natural healing. *Most people will recover well.* Only a small percentage of them will experience long-lasting psychological effects, even in the aftermath of terrible disasters. If you only learn one thing from this training, let it be this: Encourage, do not interfere with natural healing!

Summary

Communities typically go through predictable phases when disaster strikes: **pre-disaster**, in which optimism and realism are in balance; **impact**, when the reality of what is happening erodes optimism and they focus on survival for themselves and those who are closest; **heroic**, when attention shifts to the responders and people turn positive again; **disillusionment**, when optimism fades and the long-term difficulties of recovery feel overwhelming; **reconstruction**, when the "new normal" is just normal, with realism and optimism back in balance. Only a small

percent of people experience long-term psychological difficulties. Encourage, don't interfere with natural coping.

Ten: Psychological First Aid - Overview

Many versions of psychological first aid (PFA) have been around since the 1950s. Scientific evaluation is available but reading the research can be confusing because many of the papers fail to identify which PFA protocols were studied. However, over the last twenty years, several protocols have become well established and are considered "evidence informed." That means they are based on peer-reviewed research. It is the strongest endorsement science can give for this kind of curriculum. Random controlled trials, the gold standard in science, would be unethical because researchers would have to intentionally traumatize people to test. Since that won't happen (I hope) there is some argument and confusion about what is effective or potentially harmful.

The PFA material in this book draws from my experience and training with two well-established PFA protocols:

- SAFER-R, developed by Dr. George Everly, co-founder of the International Critical Incident Stress Foundation.
- The PFA curriculum developed by the National Child Trauma Support Network and the Veterans Administration National Center for PTSD, as described in its free, downloadable Field Operations Manual.

Psychological First Aid is part of the "continuum of care" of Critical Incident Stress Management (CISM). If you have taken the CERT Disaster Psychology module, you have gotten an overview of the components of CISM[2].

- Pre-incident planning and preparation – that's what you are doing right now, by reading this book. It also includes organizing teams, planning activation procedures and so forth.
- Individual support – PFA protocol are always appropriate for supporting individuals.
- Team/group support – PFA can be used to support groups. Higher levels of CISM training (defusings and debriefings, below) are designed specifically for teams.

---

[2] To learn more about CISM, go to https://icisf.org

- Referrals – at every level of the continuum of care, providers need to know how and when to make referrals to a higher level.
- Defusings and debriefings – these are interventions that are designed for groups that were a team before going through a critical incident and will work as a team afterward. Although these are described in the CERT module, *further training is required to lead them.*
- Spiritual support – pastors, ministers, lay religious counselors such as Stephen Ministers and others.
- Family support – counselors and others who have specific training and experience helping families. PFA can be used to support families.
- Therapy – licensed clinicians offer deeper care.
- In-patient, on-site care – the ultimate intensive care comes from checking into a residential facility.

The continuum of care only works if providers know when and how to make referrals. Like the emergency room doctor who knows when to refer a patient to a surgeon, cardiologist, or other specialist, you need to know when to refer. In general, if people seem to still be in need of support after you have spent a couple of hours in a couple of sessions with them, it's time to refer them.

Reading this book is unlikely to fully prepare you to deliver psychological first aid, unless you already have some kind of crisis intervention training and experience. Ideally, take a class from a qualified instruction, including role-playing, so that you have a chance to try out some of these techniques in a setting where you will receive feedback from someone experienced. Although you may use these skills in your everyday life, you should only respond to a disaster as part of a recognized team that is integrated into the overall response.

When I introduce crisis intervention to people I'm supporting, often one of the first things I usually say is, "I'm not here to fix this or make it better." That's a reminder to myself as much as it is information for them. When people have strong emotional reactions, it is almost always due to a situation that felt out of control, which cannot be fixed or made better. If someone has died, there is no "fixing" that.

- Stay within the scope of your training and experience. Never, ever push, poke, prod or otherwise pressure people to talk about their experiences. Invite, invite, invite! This also means you should never apply psychological labels, such as "symptoms," "disorders," etc.
- Take the word "should" and its synonyms "ought to," "need to," etc. out of your vocabulary during psychological first aid. Encourage those in crisis to

do the same, which helps them regain a sense of control.

- Listen, listen, listen. If you are talking a lot, you probably are not helping. You may be bringing your own issues into the conversation, which is rarely helpful. Allow silence. You will grow more comfortable with silence as you practice it.

- Be sensitive to culture and diversity. There is more to know that most of us can ever grasp but do your best to be aware of what might or might not be proper or acceptable. When in doubt, ask. When you make a mistake, don't defend, apologize. Take advantage of resources for cultural and diversity training and education. You'll find many online at no cost.

Do not try to make people feel better. Yes, you read that correctly. *Do not try to make people feel better.* Your presence is more powerful than any sort of "cheering up" you might offer. If your goal is to make people feel better, you probably will add to their isolation: they get the message that it's no okay to be sad, angry, frustrated, or whatever else they are feeling other than happy. Instead, aim to help people recognize and express what they *are* feeling.

Being with a group of people who are expressing difficult feelings is uncomfortable. I remind my team that if people are crying in your presence, they trust you. It is a compliment. Be honored by it. Yet also bear in mind that if they show no reactions, that may have nothing to do with you. Some people are "highly defended," meaning that they are unlikely to express their emotions in any setting.

There is only one way to get rid of bad feelings: have them. That's why it backfires when you try to make people feel better; you don't give them room to go ahead and have their difficult emotions.

Here are some of the ways that people, usually with good intentions, try and make others feel better.

- Don't use clichés or imagine that you can under-stand others' grief. Stay away from, "It could be worse," "I understand how you feel," and so forth.
- Don't remind them of what's still good in their lives. You can invite *them* to name what's still good, but that comes at the end of interventions and it needs to be their opinion, not yours.

> For a hilarious, but deeply true lesson about not trying to fix or make things better, take a look at the short video, "It's Not About the Nail." You'll find it on YouTube.

- Never urge them to "get over" or "move on" from a difficult incident. When people suffer emotional injury, they are changed forever. Life will not be the same, but that doesn't mean it won't be good again. (All three of my sib-lings have died. I won't "get over" those losses – to do so would mean forgetting them, which would be inhuman.) The best we do with these memories is figure out how to live with them.

PFA Guidelines

- Be calm, courteous, organized, and helpful, which will *show* people more than your words can tell.
- Make a compassionate human connection without intruding.
- Restore a sense of safety. Remember that the stress autopilot reacts strongly to threats. Physical safety comes first.

- Help calm survivors. Get them from feeling out-of-control to feeling in-control. One of the keys is to give up your own need for control. Invite, rather than telling people what to do, pressuring, prodding, or making decisions for them. Take

  > Don't instruct or assume. Invite and ask. Give up control where you can. For example, I never close a door for confidentiality. I ask, "Is it okay if we close the door?" It lets others know they are in charge, not me.

  control only when there is immediate danger.
- Encourage people to identify and prioritize their immediate needs. Assist as appropriate. Ask, "What is most difficult for you right now?" Realize that you may not be able to make a difference about whatever they name (which often will be "helplessness" or something similar) but keep in mind that your presence is making a difference.

- Get people out of isolation, a stress autopilot activator, and into supportive community, a renewal activator.
- Acknowledge and support their strengths and efforts to cope with the crisis.
- Provide additional information when you are certain it is accurate and helpful.
- Follow up and/or refer to other resources.
- Take care of yourself (which is why the first half of this book is about how to be more resilient).

When Offering Support[3]

DO	DON'T
Intervene based on *reactions*.	Intervene based on *what happened*.
Listen.	Advise.
Connect.	Control.
Offer and invite.	Instruct or insist.
Be patient.	Rush.
Support and normalize.	Interfere with healing.
Be real.	"Should" or "Ought to."
Accompany.	Use clichés.
Maintain confidentiality and trust.	Pressure, prod or provoke.
Allow silence.	Talk too much.
Ask "What's hitting hardest?" "What do you need right now?"	Ask "Are you okay?" or other closed-end questions.
Take care of yourself.	Ignore your own stuff.
Rely on your team, friends and family.	Fly solo or imagine you're the only one who....

---

[3] From the *Pocket Guide to Stress Management and Crisis Response*. Stress, Spirit, Science, 2017. Available on Amazon.

Summary

Many PFA protocols have been developed in recent decades, making scientific evaluations confusing and ambiguous. SAFER-R and the NCTSN/VA protocols are evidence-informed and widely used. PFA is part of the CISM "Continuum of Care," which includes planning, responses, several types of caregivers, and referrals. Stay within the scope of your training and refer people to a higher level of care when needed. Avoid the "shoulds." Listen more than you talk. Be sensitive to culture and diversity. Don't try to make people feel better. Don't use clichés. Avoid language like "moving on" or "getting over" a crisis. Work with a team rather than freelancing. Try to have background information before intervening. Be calm, courteous, organized, and helpful. Be compassionate without being intrusive. Help restore safety and calm. Encourage people to identify and prioritize their needs. Encourage them to avoid isolation. Acknowledge and support their strengths.

Provide information. Refer when needed. Take care of yourself.

.

Eleven: Delivering Psychological First Aid

Before Intervening

First, *observe*. Are survivors having strong reactions? Are they taking care of each other? Can you offer help without being intrusive or disruptive? Often, the best way to get started is to offer practical help – basic necessities they might need.

Although there may be unplanned times when your PFA skills come into play, generally do not self-deploy or freelance in emergencies. Teams

Five Ts for planning
Target – who needs help? Large, small; mixed or cohesive?
Type – of assistance needed? Interactive or informational? Families? Organization?
Timing – when, for each target?
Theme – what had impact?
Team – who are the best facilitators? How many? Special skills?

coordinate responses to avoid overlap or gaps. More importantly, you should have a team's resources available to support you, because secondary trauma happens. Your team should be knowledgeable and connected with the Incident Command System that defines how we respond to emergencies large and small.

Do your best to get accurate information about what is going on before responding, but also realize that what you hear often will be inaccurate, especially if it comes from media reports. Rumors fly during emergencies.

Physical Safety

Physical safety comes first. Before engaging in conversation, ensure that you and the people you are helping are in a safe environment. If you have responded to the scene of an emergency, *invite* them to get some distance, if only because the sights, sounds,

> **Medical Needs Questions**
> - Do you have a medical or other condition needing attention?
> - Do you need prescriptions?
> - Do you need help contacting your doctor?
> - Do you need help getting a prescription filled?

and smells are distracting. However, don't force them, unless there is an immediate threat to their safety (in which case, you may not belong there, either). Mitigate small safety problems yourself, but if there is a safety issue you are not qualified to address – threats, weapons, etc., get help from qualified responders.

Practical assistance precedes inviting people to talk about how they are doing emotionally. If they urgently need medical care, medications, food, or rest and sleep, or help with health-related issues, assist them with those first. Let them do as much as possible for themselves. If they are separated from family or pets, although you can be supportive, don't expect much of their attention until they know all are okay. If you can *safely* help

> Don't underestimate the impact of extensive damage or destruction of property – home, work, school, etc. It is natural and appropriate for people to be worried and concerned. Resist the temptation to compare these losses to life and limb. *No comparison stress shopping!*

them get information about loved ones or reunite them, do so. Our brains under stress become hungry for information, particularly when it feels as though it would give us more control of the situation.

If you need to have an adults-only conversation, parents will need know that their children are in a safe area, supervised by a trusted adult, where they can rest or play.

People may feel unsafe because they feel persecuted due to ethnicity, religion, immigration, or other status. For example, at shelter locations, although having law enforcement present for security

> Medical Red Flag – Confusion
> Disorientation or communications difficulty – "altered mental state" – often indicates a medical emergency. Check with companions or family to find out if it is their normal state. If not, or you cannot determine, seek medical help *immediately*. Do the same for anyone showing other signs of shock – pale, clammy skin, weak or rapid pulse.

ment present for security may be necessary, it also may discourage some people from coming. In situations like that, do your best to obtain a neutral location. When I can plan ahead, I'll ask where people will be most comfortable meeting, which also gives them some control.

Do your best to see that people have adequate light, eyeglasses, hearing aids, wheelchairs and other items required for addressing functional needs.

Having nothing to do can be difficult. It is okay to give people simple, safe tasks, to help their stress autopilot settle down. Working in relief centers, I sometimes make sure there are some boxes that need to be moved. Those boxes have sometimes moved back and forth multiple times!

Objective information about what is going on can help people feel safer. Such information **must** be accurate. Although some information may be upsetting, be wary of withholding it; you may break the trust that is essential to the healing relationship. The higher the stakes, the more our brain wants to know and learn. Sometimes, when the unknowns are causing stress, the best thing you can say is, "Not knowing is hard." In the aftermath of a fatality, answers are often slow in coming and sometimes never do. You

may reassure people that it is natural to hunger to know, and not knowing is hard, especially when life and limb are involved. That's the power of "acknowledgement" and you will learn more about it shortly.

Understanding how emergency responders are handling the situation to make things safer can also be reassuring. In the aftermath of terrible events, I sometimes invite police, fire, and EMS to visit schools and allow the students to explore their equipment, ask questions and learn about everything public safety does. As symbols of safety, they can be a powerful reminder that although bad things happen sometimes, we have people who are dedicated to preventing and responding to them.

Making Contact

"How are you?" is **not** a helpful way to begin any kind of crisis intervention, formal or informal. People usually automatically answer, "Fine." On my team, we joke that

"FINE" stands for Fouled up, Insecure, Neurotic, and Emotional. If they really are fine, psychological first aid isn't needed.

To engage, look for those who are seeking help, but remain alert for those who may benefit but are not approaching you. Don't interrupt their conversations. Rather than asking for information about how they are, begin by introducing yourself (name, title, and why you are there) and gently asking, "Would you like to talk for a few minutes?" If they are seated, sit with them. If you are working with children, sit or crouch so you are at eye level. Hovering over anyone is never good. Get the names of the people you are talking to, try to memorize them, and use them in conversation. If they don't want your help, you must respect that, but it is good to let them know how to get help later. That can be a bit easier if you say they might want to be able to tell others how to get aid. People often are much more willing to give others help than to accept it for themselves.

With minors, it is always a good idea to connect with parents or guardians before engaging. If that isn't possible, seek them out as soon as you are able.

Go slow. Keep things simple. Avoid jargon and clichés. Crises are messy and affect every part of people's lives, leaving them feeling overwhelmed. If you ask a broad question, such as, "What do you need?" they are likely to have a tough time coming up with one answer.

To help people regain a sense of control, offer encouragement and guidance for them to prioritize so that they can deal with just one piece at a time. "What is most important to you right now?" is a straightforward way. Or you might ask, "What is hardest for you right now?"

If you can see that they may be hungry or thirsty, offer to get them food or drinks if they are available. If they seem to be cold, offer a blanket if you can get one.

Overwhelmed people have a tough time identifying or prioritizing what they need. However, once they name what is most important or difficult, they often can come up with an answer to "What do you need the most right now?"

Notice that these questions include the words "right now." Stress takes us out of the present moment, generating anxiety about the past and worry about the future. By encouraging people to come into the present, you will help settle down the stress autopilot.

Elizabeth Weingarten, managing editor at Behavioral Scientist, developed a list of twenty questions to ask instead of "How are you doing right now?" in response to the pandemic. She also offers nine questions for taking things a step further.

- How are you taking care of yourself today?
- What part of your shelter-in-place residence have you come to appreciate the most?
- What surprising thing have you been stocking up on (that isn't toilet paper)?
- What's a story – from a book, a movie, an article, a conversation – that you've been gripped by recently? Why did it capture you?
- What habit have you started, or broken, during the quarantine?
- Which specific place in your neighborhood are you most looking forward to visiting once this is all over?
- What's the easiest part about the quarantine?
- What are some things you have realized that you don't really need?

- What's something you own that feels useful?
- What is your Covid-19 nickname/alter-ego?
- What problem—either yours, or something more global —do you wish you could solve?

Although *emotional safety* comes after physical safety, it is equally essential, starting with confidentiality. Although there are exceptions – immediate threats of harm to self or others – you must keep your conversations completely private. Confidentiality means choosing a location where no one can overhear and resisting any temptation you might feel to repeat what others say. No one should take notes, photos, or other recordings of a

Confidentiality can be a legal obligation and ethical obligation. If you work or volunteer through a health care provider, HIPAA – the *Health Information Portability and Accountability Act of 1996* – applies, with some waivers, during disaster or terrorism incidents. If you have any doubts about releasing information – even the fact that you talked to someone – check with a supervisor.

crisis intervention, ever. Avoid noise and other distractions, especially if you are working with people with disabilities, especially those who might have trouble seeing or hearing clearly, or have memory or cognitive challenges.

Here is how I ask for confidentiality: "Does everyone here agree to only take away their own story, not anyone else's?" After saying this, I take a moment to look at each person, giving them a chance to nod or say yes.

You, as the provider of psychological first aid, should say that the only information you will ever share will be what might be necessary to help people in the group obtain follow-up care. Mention the two big exceptions to confidentiality – when someone is inclined to hurt themself or another person.

No one should be present as a "guest" or observer. Only those who have been impacted by the disaster or other event should be involved. News media should never be present.

As a crisis interventionist, you should never talk to news media, to avoid even an impression that your work is anything other than completely confidential. Nor should you post anything in social media or other public places. Similarly, shield survivors from media, especially children.

Some people may want to tell their story to a reporter. Ideally, they will know enough about that journalist to have reason to trust them. When our niece's husband was killed in action, a television news reporter showed up at his parent's house, with genuine tears for their loss. He did a wonderful job of telling Wes' story. That recognition helped everyone's grief, I am certain. On the other hand, poor journalism and manipulation can make things worse, so urge survivors to be wary, especially when emotions are running high

> I turned off TV news in the spring of 2004 and don't miss it. And I was a reporter for a decade! For-profit news organizations, no matter how much they may aim for a higher mission, eventually answer to their real customers: advertisers. "Enragement is engagement," as someone observed, because getting you riled up *sells*.

(which is exactly what news media, especially television, seeks). Our team always invites people to go on a "news diet" after a difficult incident. Not only the coverage of that event is often too much, seeing news about similar ones, even weeks or months later, can be painful. I strongly urge parents with children under 10 to completely protect them from TV news coverage of emergencies and disasters.

Trust is also vital, which means you also need to be quite careful about information that you share with others. Make *certain* of the accuracy of anything you tell people when you offer psychological support. Double check. Triple check! Be utterly certain, because broken trust is difficult to earn back. I'm emphasizing this point because emergencies and disasters are powerful rumor generators as people frantically seize at anything that gives them a feeling of control. Our brains like to "fill in the gaps" during crises. Bear in mind also that our brain's "negative bias" leads us to believe and share negative information more readily. Do not be reluctant to say, "I don't know." If you think you might be able to find out, offer to do so but make no promises.

Another trust problem is the "little white lie" that is intended to make people feel better. Never do that and watch out for others. I did a death notification at a school where a police officer was telling people that their friend died quietly in bed, when that wasn't at all what happened. Unfortunately, I worsened the situation; it didn't occur to me that perhaps it wasn't true, and I repeated it. When one of the friends learned what truly happened, he scolded me angrily – and I deserved it. Double check, no matter who the source is.

Talking about stressful things is often helpful, but each person must have freedom to choose when, where, and who they talk to. Never, ever push, prod, or pressure others to talk about a potentially traumatic event. By doing so, you probably will make things worse for them, not better.

Part of my introduction at every crisis intervention is: "It's okay if this isn't the right time and place for you to talk. It is perfectly okay to sit here quietly. Everyone has the right to choose who, when, and where to talk about difficult things." Notice that this puts *them* in control, not me. I'm fairly certain that by giving people that control, they talk *more* than if I didn't say that. Giving others control is essential to creating emotional safety. When people go through a critical incident, they are left feeling helpless and out of control. Remember, a big part of your job is to help get them from feeling out-of-control back to in-control.

I was impressed by a police officer who showed how to give others control in a simple, yet powerful way. After a sudden and traumatic death in a home, he was talking to a survivor who was standing and pacing around. "Would you like to sit down?" he asked. He asked that question, gently, repeatedly, over the course of forty-five minutes, when the person finally was ready to sit down. I've had people faint in front of me in situations like that, but I still would not ever pressure someone to sit. You will probably find your own desire for control in a chaotic situation a bit difficult to notice and resist. But do it. You are there to help others regain control, not to take it away from them.

My usual introduction includes, "I'm not here to fix this or make it better." Truth is, I cannot. The only "fix" for traumatic incidents would be to turn back the clock and get a do-over. That's beyond my power and I often say just that. I also say those words to remind myself to let go of the problem-solving, action-oriented person I am when working in fire and EMS, where my job most certainly is to take control and fix the problem. But psychological first aid is not like that. Your goal needs to be to help others regain their sense of control and their connections to community.

Explain the purpose of psychological first aid (although you don't have to use that name for it, which might be intimidating). It is not counseling or therapy; its purpose is to help people return to their normal level of functioning faster after a high-stress or traumatic event. Tell them that your biggest goal is to help them learn to support each other, in the coming days, weeks, months, or even years of recovery and healing. Remember, "You are each other's best support," is a powerful reminder of what psychology has learned about social support.

To recap, emotional safety means confidentiality, trust, presence, encouraging social support, and not yielding to the urge to "fix" them.

The third dimension of safety is spiritual. This means respecting others' beliefs, values, and priorities. A crisis is not merely the wrong time to impose your values or faith on others, doing so is abusive, in my opinion. As a fire chaplain working with public safety agencies, I am forbidden – and properly so – from any sort of promotion or proselytizing of my own beliefs. The same goes for your political, social, scientific, and any other such opinions you might be tempted to share. You can respond to others' thoughts and feelings about faith and such, but you must not lead them there. Sensitive and potentially divisive subjects are rarely appropriate in a group setting; be wary of going there even in one-on-one encounters.

Under spiritual safety, I also put "Be kind rather than nice." Don't be nice? Yes, don't be nice, be kind. The difference is that when we are nice, our intention is usually to make people like us. Aim to set that aside. Be kind – give people gifts they cannot repay you. For me, this means somethings saying things that might sound a bit tough if they were not said in kindness. A good example is this: "Your life will never be the same." Although that might seem harsh, since it sounds like the opposite of "everything will be all right," (which you should never say) it is a powerful *acknowledgement* of the impact of disaster or another major incident. I often follow it up with something like, "That doesn't mean your life won't be good again, but it won't be the same."

Remember that for the people you are accompanying as a provider of psychological first aid, life is not good, not okay, right now. As odd as it might sound, they need acknowledgement more than reassurance. Even children, who certainly do need reassurance, benefit from gentle acknowledgements, such as "This is scary right now, isn't it?" Knowing it is okay to be scared – or angry, sad, frustrated, etc. – helps. That is kindness even though it might not feel so nice.

To summarize, creating spiritual safety means always being sensitive to and respecting others' beliefs and values, refraining from any kind of judgment or advice. Your role is compassion, much more than guidance.

Stabilization

Those who are showing signs of acute distress are your highest priority – disoriented, confused, frantic, agitated, panicky, withdrawn, "shut down," highly irritable or angry, or exceptionally worried. This does not automatically mean they need a higher level of care; all of these are normal and natural responses to crisis.

If you do nothing else, simply being a calm and comforting presence is often enough. Psychological research shows that knowing someone cares – even a stranger – helps them to cope. Your presence alone, the fact that you have taken the time to show up and be with struggling people, makes a difference – even if they don't wish to talk to you.

"Would you like to walk with me?" is a simple invitation that can do wonders. If you sense resistance to talking, you might also reassure them that it will be okay to just walk quietly. If others are open to it, the grounding, breathing, and relaxation exercises from Chapter Four can help lower the stress response[4]. As usual, invite without pressuring. Don't tell people what you think they need; let them tell you. (If you use the grounding technique of scanning surroundings, stay away from focusing on an emergency scene.)

If someone is having an extreme reaction and unwilling or unable to accept your invitation of assistance, consider locating family or friends to be with them, if possible. Remember to focus on the individual's greatest concerns. Do not invite or urge them to calm down or try and talk them out of what they are feeling. Not only do those not work, they often make things worse by decreasing their sense of control.

---

[4] Also see "Tips for Relaxation" in the NCTSN/VA Psychological First Aid Field Manual.

Simply asking them what is going on for them is far better. Even if they don't respond, you have let them know you are available and care, which makes a difference. Give them some space or offer something they can do to help. With time, they are more likely to respond.

Bring your curiosity to crisis intervention. It is a powerful tool when it is the right *kind* of curiosity. Set aside your curiosity about what happened or what it was like to experience the disaster or crisis. Show up with curiosity about the *people*, rather than the incident, and how it was

> If you are *curious* to learn more about these two kinds of curiosity, search online for articles about "deprivation" versus "interest" curiosity.

for them to go through it. Don't ask people to tell the story of what happened to them. If they volunteer that kind of information, resist your natural desire to know further details. Your stress autopilot will urge you to learn from their experience, but that will not be helpful to them. Instead, invite others to let you know how it has been to experience the crisis, through their eyes, their mind, their heart.

Identify Needs and Priorities

Situations in which you need to take control are rare; most of the time, you will be aiming to help reduce survivors' feelings of helplessness by putting them in control as much as you can. To accomplish that, you need to learn their needs and priorities. Throughout delivery of psychological first aid, you will be gathering and evaluating information.

> The NCTSN/VA PFA Field Manual has worksheets to help record your observations ("Survivor Current Needs") and how you responded ("PFA Components Provided"). If you use them, fill them out in private, after your encounter, and treat them as highly confidential.

- Need for referral.
- Further services.
- Need for follow-up with your team.

- Helpful psychological first aid skills.

Although reactions are more important than what happened, learning what survivors experienced can give insight into how much it affected them. As they talk about what they went through, you may see new reactions. *Do not try to elicit an emotional response.* (I have repeated this guidance several times because it helps to ensure that you will do no harm.)

Ask for permission to ask some questions about what they went through. If they are open, you may gently ask things like these, but remember not to pressure or probe.

- Where were you as it happened?
- Were you injured?
- Did you see anyone else get hurt?
- How scary was it for you?
- Who else are you worried about? Is anyone missing? (People and pets!)

The more people talk about feeling helpless or out of control, the more likely they are to need time and support to recover from the crisis.

Stay away from "why" questions, which typically activate the "defend and distance" response, raising their stress level. No one needs to defend their decisions or actions during a crisis.

If they are eager to talk in detail about their experience, don't interrupt, but invite them to give you basic information now and explain that additional services will be available. *Psychological debriefing, in which people are invited to go through their story in more detail, requires a higher level of training and experience.*

Find out if someone close to survivors was seriously injured or killed in the emergency. If so, use your skills to comfort, connect them with social support and grief intervention as available. Offer a follow up.

Recall that our brains are often hungry for information when we are under high stress. Ask what might be helpful – information about what happened, what they need to do now (especially for their physical safety), or what emergency responders are doing. If you can *safely* get *reliable* information, do so and provide it.

Check in on availability of social support. Ask if survivors have family, friends, a church or other institution that might be able to help them get through this. If their network is lacking, help them to connect with supportive people and organizations. Tell them that resilience correlates most strongly to social support and suggest that this is going to be a good time for them to build up their network. If you are speaking to a group, such as a family or co-workers, suggest that they can be each other's best support.

Substance abuse problems can be aggravated by high stress events. Ask individuals, in private, if they have increased their use of alcohol or other drugs since the crisis, or perhaps are experiencing withdrawal. Ask if they have had past problems with substance abuse. If you see a potential current issue, offer information and referrals to appropriate resources. In a group setting, you can give information and invite people to talk to you individually if they have concerns. If you are not sure where to send someone, refer them to a medical care provider. The NCTSN/VA PFA Field Manual includes a handout, *Alcohol, Medication, and Drug Use after Disasters.* SAMHSA, the Substance Abuse and Mental Health Administration, offers many resources, including a treatment directory, brochures, and other handouts.

Past trauma and stress, including grief, can amplify people's reaction to a crisis, especially if it has similarities. Let survivors know this is normal. Ask if they have been through a disaster or similar crisis before. Ask if they have had someone close die. If you see that they are

> Check for priorities you may have missed. "Do you have concerns that we haven't talked about?"

having a strong reaction, give them information and offer follow up.

Once you have identified needs, discuss a plan with priorities. Let people do as much for themselves as they can. Assist as you are able, but if there are many people needing help, it may be more important to connect them with others who can address the concerns you have identified. Of course, in a disaster, some things often must wait. Let people know that delays are normal – and frustrating!

Acknowledge and Normalize

During and after high-stress situations, people often wonder if they are going crazy. As survivors describe their physical, social, and spiritual stress responses, reassure them that they are having natural reactions to a very abnormal event. In the first month or so after a true critical incident, all reactions, other than serious urges to hurt others or themselves, are considered normal. Telling them so, which acknowledges and normalizes the emotions, helps reduce the natural fear that comes from having unfamiliar thoughts and feelings, diminishing the associated stress response.

As you acknowledge and normalize reactions, if people respond by saying something such as, "It was a relief just to know that I'm not the only one," consider that a success.

Some people and groups will be put off if you mention emotions directly. For example, I was in CISM training with a group of firefighters when one of them, half-joking, asked the instructor to "Stop dropping f-bombs," explaining that he meant "feelings." Removing the label helps. My favorite way is to ask something like, "How did you find yourself reacting?"

Many people are reluctant to say what they are thinking and feeling out of fear of seeming different, strange, or all too often, weak. A big part of crisis intervention is creating a pressure-free "safety zone" for them to voice what's really going on – if they want to.

Active Listening Techniques
- Ask open-ended questions:
  - *Would you like to tell me more about that?*
  - *How was that for you?*
  - *What is hitting hardest?*
  - *What do you need right now?*
  - *How would you do that?*
- One question at a time, listen to replies.
- Repeat key information back for confirmation.
  - *It sounds like you are saying...*
  - *It seems to me that you are...*
  - *Am I understanding you right, that...*
- Say when you don't understand, ask for clarification.
- Acknowledge emotions.
  - *No wonder (or of course) you feel...*
  - *I can see that you are angry/frustrated/sad/etc.*
- Normalize reactions.
  - *You are having a natural reaction to a very abnormal experience.*
  - *Many people feel that way (or have those kind of thoughts) after going through something like this.*
  - *I hear that from many other people, too.*
- Paraphrase/summarize thoughts and emotions.

At this phase of offering psychological first aid, your understanding of natural reactions will help you respond to what you are hearing, *but not to volunteer information about reactions*. When you are inexperienced at crisis intervention, you are likely to feel like throwing a lot of information at survivors quickly. **Do not do that!** The purpose of the following material is to *help you recognize* normal reactions to stress and trauma. Later, in Step 7, you will offer information about what kind of reactions they may have after you are gone. At first, however, when you hear someone report these reactions, reassure them that these are normal or natural reactions.

Signals of physical ("fight or flight") stress reactions:

- Craving carbohydrates, gastrointestinal and digestive issues.
- Anxiety.
- Headaches.
- Fatigue, low energy.
- Hyperactivity, adrenaline-seeking behavior, including risk-taking (which you should normalize, but discourage).
- Increased drug, alcohol craving and use (normalize the cravings, discourage acting on them).
- Disturbed sleep ("tired and wired").

Signals of social/mental ("defend and distance") stress reactions:

- "Is this really happening?"
- Denial – "I'm FINE."
- Moody, irritable, angry, frustrated, withdrawn.
- Distrust, suspicion.
- Binary, us-or-them; "possibility" thinking.

- Memory and concentration difficulties.
- Hungry for information, control – rumors, conspiracies. (More on this in the last chapter.)

Signals of spiritual ("selfish or survivalist") stress reactions:

- Lost perspective, tunnel vision.
- Hoarding.
- Altered sense of time.
- Moral, ethical changes or lapses.
- Struggle with meaning and purpose.

You can acknowledge and normalize reactions by telling people that a lot of other people are feeling or have felt the same way. Reflect the emotions you notice behind their words – "You sound frustrated (or sad, angry, or whatever emotion you notice)."

Feeling guilty, responsible, or pointing fingers at others for allowing or failing to prevent harm are normal reactions. If there is someone to blame – including ourselves – that answers our stress autopilot's desire for control. It wants to reject the idea of random bad things happening because that would mean we have no control. In other words, to that part of our brains, the illusion of control is more satisfying than the reality of terrible random things.

When you hear someone express guilt or shame, never contradict them. They feel what they feel. Instead, reflect what you heard, with words such as these: "It sounds like you are being very hard on yourself." "It is normal and natural for people to feel like they should have done more to stop this from happening (or afterward)."

Invite them to consider how else they might look at the situation. I often do this by asking, "If your friend had gone through the same thing, what would you say to them?" Very often, they realize they are being harder on themselves than others. That question helps them get some distance so they can be gentler with themselves. I often urge them to do exactly that with a phrase I've mentioned more than once in this book: Be gentle with yourself (an ongoing motto of my crisis intervention team). Self-compassion is powerful.

If you know reliable facts about what happened that might reduce guilt, offer them as clarification. Let them know that even though they may feel as though they are to blame, that doesn't make it true.

Invite (but don't pressure) survivors to "re-frame" persistent thoughts, blaming, disturbing memories, and other ways they find their brains replaying a critical incident. Acknowledge that such intrusive thoughts and emotions are normal and offer the idea that learning from bad situations is how our brains earn their paycheck,

> **Positive Re-Framing**
> Think about a negative situation in terms of potential benefits – a lesson to be learned, opportunity created by crisis, etc.

so to speak. Our ability to learn from experience is what makes humans survive and thrive. Explain that very often, when we can find or make meaning from the crisis, the brain settles down quite a bit.

From Isolation to Community

In the long run, you rarely if ever will be the most important support for people who have gone through a disaster or other crisis. It is better if you are not, because their own social support network can be available long after you are gone. Research repeatedly shows that social support correlates to resilience better than any other factor.

> Help people avoid isolation while respecting the need for solitude at times. The stress autopilot in our brains wants to know that we are not alone, not the only one struggling. A genuine "Me, too," especially from a peer, is strong medicine.

"You are each other's best support" is a phrase that our Bay Area CISM Team often repeats. No one understands what it is like to survive a crisis better than those who also went through it – or people who have been through something similar. It is natural for survivors to feel deeply bonded sometimes. Although empathy does not require understanding, those who truly can understand are special.

A big part of your job, when offering psychological first aid, is to encourage people to plug into and/or build up their own social support network. *You* also need such support, if only to help you deal with the secondary trauma that is inevitable when you empathize or identify with those in crisis. That is why the first half of this book is about what makes *you* resilient. You can't give away what you don't have!

Following a loss, people inevitably sometimes feel isolated, even from close family members, because each grief journey is different. When one is having a good day, another might be deep in sorrow. Let people know that this is normal. It becomes much easier to accept these differences when people feel that it is okay to talk about where they are, without expectations. When no one talks about their grief, everyone wonders if they are the only one hurting; that sense of isolation makes the grief more difficult. Urge them to be kind and gentle with others as well as themselves; the journey is complex and unpredictable.

Human beings are wired for life in community, even though it can be difficult. "Self-reliance" is mostly myth; no one becomes self-reliant on their own and no one is entirely self-reliant. We are more interdependent than in-dependent. Giving and receiving the blessings of commu-nity, especially after crisis, helps us to heal and grow.

Genuine connection to others creates a safety net and opportunities to do things that are impossible when we operate solo.

- Fear for your physical safety diminishes because you know there are people who will provide you with necessities; helping others with their material needs reassures you that you also will have enough for yourself.
- Acceptance as you are, rather than as others think you should be, eases feelings of guilt and shame; accepting others just as they are helps you to be less hard on yourself.
- Knowing you are not the only one struggling with difficult thoughts and feelings is reassuring. Letting

others know they are not alone does the same for them and lets you know you are valued.

- Groups can solve problems, rise to challenges, and seize opportunities that would be impossible for individuals; being in community thus yields hope. A group's knowledge, skills, and perspective is far broader than any of its members. We can overcome each other's blind spots.

Make it a priority to help survivors reconnect with their closest sources of support – family, close friends, neighbors, religious community, etc. If they are unable to reach usual sources of support, encourage them to connect with support that is available – you and your team, other disaster responders, other survivors. Whenever possible, allow and encourage survivors to support each other. Anything supportive you might say or do will have a greater impact if it comes from a peer – someone who has gone through the same or similar experience as a survivor. Do your best to match people with others who might be able to assist, such as connecting the elderly with younger people. Children should be grouped with others of similar age, with age-appropriate games or other activities.

People may be naturally hesitant to ask for support from others. They may not know what is available, what they need, or believe no one can understand or help. Asking for help might feel like weakness or an imposition on others. The purpose of the "no comparison stress shopping" guideline is to help people avoid minimizing their own needs. Trusting others is especially difficult after trauma. You can reassure them that no one gets through crises well on their own; giving and receiving support are healing.

Invite survivors to talk about what kind of support would be most helpful. Ask, "What has helped you in the past?" Invite them to consider who they might turn to, how and when to approach those people. As always, give people clear permission to not talk about what they have been through. Let them know that people often instinctively want to be with those we feel close to – that's the oxytocin-driven "tend and befriend" renewal response – but each person has the right to decide what to talk about and who to talk to.

In one culture, when someone dies, people respond by saying, "I stand beside you." Often that is enough. When my younger sister suddenly died, a friend and neighbor did that for me. He said, "I have no idea what to do, just let me know what you'd like." That was perfect. A quiet walk with someone who isn't trying to make things better can be powerful.

When you sense that survivors are concerned that others might pressure them to talk when they don't wish to, offer them this response, "Not right now," which is easier to say than "No." Assure them that they do not owe their story to anyone, especially those who are motivated by the "wrong" kind of curiosity (what happened, v. how it was for them).

As you offer guidance on receiving support, bear in mind that you are also showing and telling how to give support – which is at least equally healing. Your *example* may be the most precious gift they take away.

> When possible, have practical information about evacuation centers, shelters, local assistance centers, urgent care, hospitals, 24-hour pharmacies, meal services, access, reunification processes, functional needs assistance, chaplains and clergy available, and so forth.

Encouragement – Providing Information

Be prepared to give people *accurate and reliable* information about the crisis – what happened and what is being done in response. Remember, *not knowing is hard.* Talk to them, but when possible, also give them printed handouts they can take with them. Stick to information that is helpful and understandable given their situation and abilities. Be wary of overwhelming them.

Never begin by handing them papers. Aim to first make a personal connection. Listen and address their greatest concerns. Only describe resources that you are certain are available to them.

Be ready to use the words, "I don't know, but I will try to find out." If practical, guide them to get information on their own, which has the added benefit of giving

> Useful information for survivors of disaster:
> - Options for what to do next.
> - Services available or coming.
> - Facts about the incident.
> - Typical stress reactions.
> - How to activate renewal reactions.
> - How to care for others.

them something to do. For example, if they are concerned about insurance claims, you might direct them toward United Policyholders, an insurance customer advocacy group that nearly always responds to disasters. If they are overwhelmed by the logistics of recovery, you might connect them with a case manager, often provided by organizations such as Catholic Charities and the Red Cross.

Let people know that reactions can surface in many ways, for a long time after a high-stress event. The Centre for Living with Dying in Santa Clara, California, has created the following widely used one-page handout. The purpose of this type of handout is to help survivors realize that their reactions are natural.

143

Reactions in the Aftermath of a Critical Incident

A critical incident is any event that causes unusually strong reactions in the responding personnel or survivors. These reactions/responses can occur immediately or in a delayed fashion.

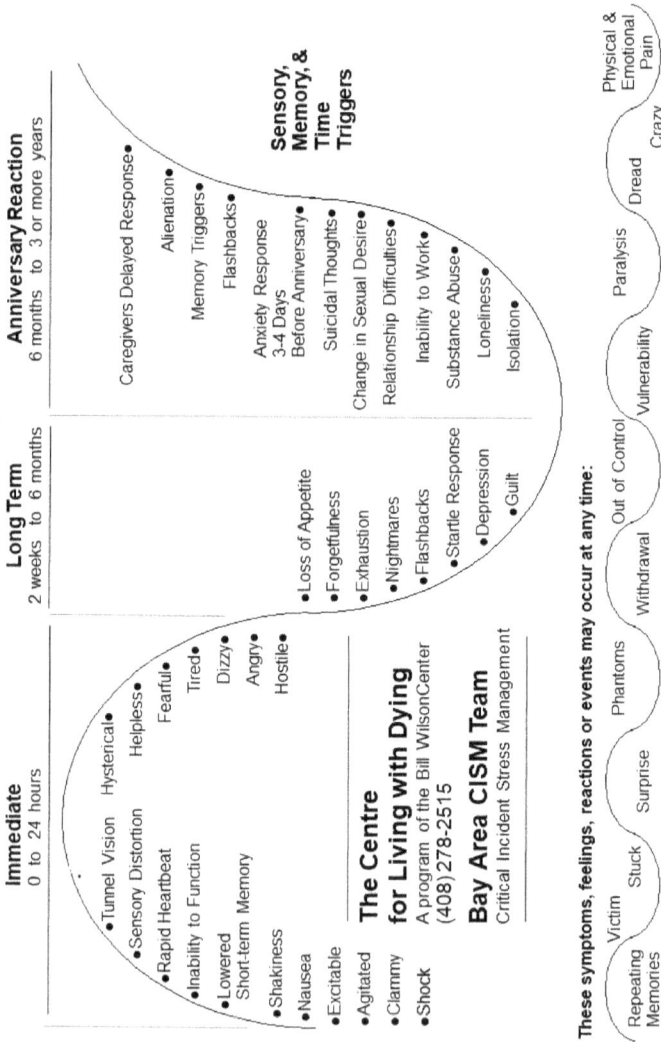

Immediate
0 to 24 hours

- Tunnel Vision
- Sensory Distortion
- Rapid Heartbeat
- Inability to Function
- Lowered Short-term Memory
- Shakiness
- Nausea
- Excitable
- Agitated
- Clammy
- Shock
- Hysterical
- Helpless
- Fearful
- Tired
- Dizzy
- Angry
- Hostile

Long Term
2 weeks to 6 months

- Loss of Appetite
- Forgetfulness
- Exhaustion
- Nightmares
- Flashbacks
- Startle Response
- Depression
- Guilt

Anniversary Reaction
6 months to 3 or more years

- Caregivers Delayed Response
- Alienation
- Memory Triggers
- Flashbacks
- Anxiety Response 3-4 Days Before Anniversary
- Suicidal Thoughts
- Change in Sexual Desire
- Relationship Difficulties
- Inability to Work
- Substance Abuse
- Loneliness
- Isolation

Sensory, Memory, & Time Triggers

The Centre for Living with Dying

A program of the Bill WilsonCenter
(408) 278-2515

Bay Area CISM Team
Critical Incident Stress Management

These symptoms, feelings, reactions or events may occur at any time:

Repeating Memories — Victim — Stuck — Surprise — Phantoms — Withdrawal — Out of Control — Paralysis — Dread — Physical & Emotional Pain — Crazy — Vulnerability — Loneliness

Let survivors know to expect the road forward to be twisty and complicated. Recovery is never a straight line; it is more like spaghetti. Urge them to never interpret a temporary setback as a permanent character flaw.

The National Center for PTSD offers a two-page handout that can help you become familiar with the types of reactions people may experience after a traumatic experience. Be familiar with these, but always bear in mind that most people will recover well on their own. Here is a summary of the four types of reactions.

- Re-experiencing – intrusive memories, nightmares and flashbacks, strong physical reactions.
- Avoidance – not talking or avoiding reminders.
- Numbing – feeling detached, losing interest, forgetting, and other kinds of withdrawal, increased use of alcohol or other depressant drugs.

- Activation – feeling keyed up, jumpy, irritable, easily startled, on alert, difficulty concentrating or sleeping, increased use of stimulant drugs.

Use your knowledge of reactions to reassure people that they are not going crazy or weak when these happen. Invite them to use renewal activities – breathing, grounding, yoga, prayer, music, nature, companionship, and so forth, to help quiet the reactions.

As you educate people about reactions, let them know that it is normal to experience reminders that trigger memories and the way they felt during the crisis. My team sometimes calls these "land mines." These can be sights, sounds, smells, stories, locations, times of day or year, feelings, or other situations. Their current crisis may have triggered reminders of previous ones.

Crisis can create insecurities that make recovery challenging: loss of a home or possessions, financial difficulties, health problems, isolation from friends and family, dealing with government, insurance, and other bureaucracies.

8. Recovery and Referrals

It is essential that you understand and recognize when to refer people to care outside of your training and experience. You are like the paramedic who knows when a patient needs to be transported to an emergency room for definitive care, or the emergency room physician who knows when to refer to a specialist.

The "continuum of care" only works when caregivers at each level are knowledgeable and sensitive to making proper referrals. It starts with you, the first aid provider in the field. It may include counselors, therapists, physicians, and ultimately, in-patient psychiatric care.

Referrals might be to a therapist or emergency room, and in some situations law enforcement may be needed. Here are situations that call for urgent or immediate referral.

- When a person's emotional state is worsening, especially if rapid.
- Any time domestic, child, or elder abuse is suspected or observed. State laws vary, but you may be a "mandated reporter," legally obligated to report such situations.
- If medication needed to stabilize a person.
- Those with long-term coping difficulties – still struggling significantly a month or more after the initial incident.

- For children, some developmental regression is normal, but if they are showing significant issues, make a referral.
- Refer anyone who requests one.

You must get help for anyone who is threatening to hurt themselves or others. If you are at risk, disengage and notify law enforcement. There are three levels of urgency to this type of referral, based on their intention, plan, and resources to carry out the plan. In all cases, first invite them to self-refer, which keeps them in control and helps reduce the stress activation.

- First Priority: They have an intention, a plan, and the resources to carry it out. In this case, you must get help immediately and do not leave them alone. Accompany them to a hospital or other facility. If they refuse to self-refer, think of your situation this way: they are not being mature enough to take responsibility for their own life, it is now in your hands. Take that responsibility seriously. This is a "Call 911" situation if nothing else works.

- **Second Priority:** They have an intention and a plan, but not the resources. In this case, help make an *immediate* appointment.
- **Third Priority:** They only have an intention, without a plan or resources. In this case, help them make an appointment in the next few days with a clinician or other professional.

There are many other kinds of referrals. The more you know about what is available, the better you can serve survivors. Services include:

- Mental health.
- Medical.
- Social support.
- Child welfare.
- Schools.

- Drug and alcohol support.

You may also refer them to their own social support network, clergy, mentors, or other kinds of counselors and support.

To make a referral, work with the person to agree on a summary of the reasons and plan. This will help ensure that both of you understand and agree on why and how the referral will happen. Let them know the options they have and ask what thoughts or feelings they have about the plan. Give them the referral information in writing. If possible, especially if the need seems urgent help them make an appointment.

You generally cannot legally refer children for care without their parents' consent except in an emergency. Engaging a parent or other trusted adult will make them more likely to follow through on referrals. The more information you can provide (with permission) with the referral, the easier you can make it for them, so they don't have to retell their story to get started.

Ensure that elderly survivors have referral information for medical care, senior services, and other relevant social services, such as Meals on Wheels, housing, and transportation.

When you are able, make personal introductions, especially if you have an established relationship with the person or agency to which you are referring. This will help survivors feel a sense of continuity as they recover from the crisis.

Twelve: Special Situations

Support via Phone, Video, or Text

Providing psychological first aid via telephone, video, or text messages presents additional challenges. Important emotional cues are missing or diminished, especially those that make renewal activation contagious, such as facial expressions, eye contact, and touch.

When calling someone for the first time, introduce yourself casually – your name and the organization you represent. Find out where they are (in case you need to have emergency services respond). Expect to need to repeat yourself – stress makes our attention wander. Before diving into conversation, ask, "Is this a good time to talk?" Also ask how much time they have, so that you won't have to break off suddenly.

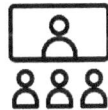

To ensure that people feel that electronic conversations are confidential, there should be no background voices or uninvolved people visible. On video, use a calming background if you can.

On the phone, when people are talking, let them know you are listening by offering small sounds of acknowledgement. It is more difficult to allow silence when you cannot see people but do your best to allow it. If it seems to go on for a long time, gently ask if the person would like to let you know what was happening.

If you have to leave a message for someone, remember that it may not be confidential. Leave your name and who referred you, but do not say *why* you are calling. Only say more if the person you are calling has already assured you that their messages are confidential.

Never, ever, multi-task while offering support remotely. The people you are helping will sense that they don't have your full attention.

Sneaky Stresses

I mentioned that the first part of this book is about resilience because you can't give away what you don't have. It is stressful to provide psychological first aid. Empathy, the very quality that will make you effective at supporting others, makes you vulnerable to secondary trauma. You are an empathetic person (you would not be reading this book if you were not), which is necessary to provide care, but also means that you will, to some extent, absorb and feel the stress and trauma of the people you encounter.

Secondary trauma can happen when you are exposed to people who have been traumatized, by hearing disturbing descriptions of traumatic events by a survivor, or people inflicting cruelty on one another. Symptoms of secondary trauma are similar to those of Post-Traumatic Stress Disorder.

Psychologists call this "vicarious" or "secondary" trauma, and it is certainly real. You will need to do the things that activate your own renewal. The more often you do crisis intervention and the more intense the situations are, the more renewal activation you will need. Remember, renewal is "rest and digest," "tend and befriend," and "pause and plan." You'll be doing those things with those you care for, but do them for yourself, too. Secondary trauma can be easy to deny: "It didn't happen to me." However, for some parts of your brain, it is very much as if it *did* happen to you.

Affiliation can amplify the emotions that you absorb from others. Affiliation is straightforward: the more connected you are to those who have gone through a high-stress event, the more strongly you may feel what they are feeling. Family is usually the most powerful affiliation, especially parent-child relationships. But almost any kind of connection can

have this effect – co-workers, co-members of any kind of group, neighbors, and so forth.

I helped lead crisis intervention following a multiple murder/suicide at a dealership where we had bought a truck a few months earlier. That might seem like a thin connection but sitting at the same table where we signed the purchase papers, I was feeling a lot more of the employees' pain than I usually do.

Identification can be difficult to recognize. When the victims of a critical incident resemble you or someone you care about, you are likely to feel more of their pain. For example, a firefighter who has a ten-year-old son is likely to feel a lot of emotion after responding to a critical injury or death of a ten-year-old boy. If that child was wearing clothing that resembles their son's, that will amplify the vicarious feelings even more, along with any other resemblances.

Identification can be most difficult to acknowledge when you talk to someone who resembles you in a way that you prefer not to acknowledge. My most profound experience of this came when I spoke with a teenager who later turned out to be a suspect in his parents' murders. After a few days of the conversation bothering me, I finally realized that his feelings resembled mine when I was a teenager, which felt embarrassing to admit. However, once I acknowledged it to myself, it was easy to let go.

When you that your brain wants to replay a situation, remember that it's doing so for a good reason: your brain wants you to learn something from it. Sometimes the lesson will be concrete, but sometimes our brains just need us to create meaning from the difficult experience.

Triggers can also sneak up on you. Sights, sounds, smells, calendar dates, and other reminders of a high-stress event can make it feel as if it is happening again. For example, a police officer who served in Iraq told me that every time he drives past an asphalt factory, the smell takes him back to the desert when oil wells were on fire. Sometimes triggers are that obvious, but they also can be difficult to see.

Any time you notice that you are feeling tense or anxious but unsure why, it is good to stop for a moment and allow your intuition to speak. Are you in a situation that is reminding you of a tough time? Remember that your brain will do that. It is urging you to learn from or create meaning out of the experience. That doesn't mean it is always easy to settle your mind, but you will find that you can relax a bit by simply reminding yourself that it is normal and in the long run helpful for our brains to do this.

As you assist others, let them know that these "sneaky stressors" happen and are normal.

Groups

The same PFA techniques you use with individuals also apply to groups, such as families or co-workers. Here is some additional guidance.

- Give everyone permission to remain silent. However, I also tell them that if they *choose* to speak and name a thought or feeling that some else in the group is also having, that is helpful. In a group, as always, never pressure anyone to talk. I also often say, "You'll hear people say that talking helps. That's true, but it has to be when you are ready and with people you feel safe with. If now isn't the right time, that's perfectly okay." I urge people to follow that advice with one another, too.

  > A genuine "Me, too" is powerful, especially when it comes from a peer rather than from a leader or facilitator.

- Stay focused on the entire group's needs and concerns. Encourage them to discuss how they might cope with their immediate issues. You may encourage them to share what has worked for them in the past when they were under a lot of stress. You may offer an example of what has worked for you, but *don't tell your story.* Say something like, "When I went through a very stressful time..."
- Gently steer people way from complaining.
- Stay alert for those who need follow up care and don't allow them to dominate the conversations. Instead, offer to meet with them individually after the group session.
- Stay calm, collected, and compassionate. You are serving as a model for those you are helping.

Missing People and Pets

Not knowing – or *seeing* – that loved ones are okay activates high stress, indeed. We are wired deep down to look after and care for those we feel connected to, especially children. Normal reactions range from denial to anger, guilt, and blame. Some may insist that the person is going to be fine; others may criticize authorities for not doing enough, or for prohibiting them from entering into a danger zone to help search. People may argue with each other's thoughts and reactions; reassure them that it is normal for them to be in different places, but underneath the reactions, everyone shares concern.

As I have emphasized, your job is not to make them feel better; their pain is important. Do all that you can to help them connect with information that helps. As always, listen to their hopes and fears, even though you may not be able to do anything to help make contact. Sometimes, you may be able to arrange for them to enter a low-risk area accompanied by a first responder.

Children need to be shielded from disturbing and potentially confusing investigation activities, such as interviews or evidence collection. If children must be interviewed, someone with professional training should either do the interview or be present. It is okay for parents to share their concern that the person may have died.

Forgiveness and Punishment, Justice and Revenge

Intentional acts – terrorism, murder, etc., and sometimes even accidental ones, bring up strong emotions, typically influenced by religious and cultural beliefs and practices. Some survivors may feel that forgiveness must happen quickly. Others may believe just as strongly that the act must never be forgiven or that justice or revenge must be swift and proportional.

Never debate survivors' beliefs. Acknowledge strong feelings, but also urge them to be gentle with themselves and others on these issues. Invite them to take some time before acting. Rushing into forgiveness often leads to stuffed-down emotions; rushing into judgement invites regrets. When people speak and act as if they have no choice about these things, invite them to consider that they may. Remember that when we are stressed, we get "tunnel vision." Taking a breath, not hurrying, gives them a chance to regain perspective.

> Justice hurried is justice buried.
>
> Justice delayed is justice denied.

Forgiveness can be an important part of healing. Invite people to consider that it has two parts, the decision, which may be based in faith or psychology, and the emotional process, which inevitably takes time.

Frederic Luskin, author of *Forgive for Good*, teaches that to forgive, people need to know exactly how they feel, be able to tell that story and share it with others. He emphasizes that forgiveness is all about finding peace, not reconciling with a person who hurt you. Luskin offers a powerful nine-step process for forgiveness. Over the years, I have referred many people to his books and videos when I have seen that they were stuck in what he calls a "grievance story." I've been there myself, unaware until a friend pointed out that I was repeating an unchanging tale of pain, imagining that sharing it was helpful. As I wrote earlier, sharing your story can be healing, but not unless you gain new insights and re-write it in healthier ways.

Cultures and Diversity

Be sensitive to cultural differences, especially regarding how close to stand to others, how much eye contact to make, or whether it is okay to touch another person. Never seek to provoke an emotional reaction. Not only is that outside of your scope of practice, in some cultures public displays of emotion are seen as weakness. Seek guidance from those who they regard as formal or informal leaders, in groups from families to entire communities.

My most intense exposure to cultural differences came in 1990, when I responded to the devastating earthquake in Haiti. Although I had studied Haitian history, culture, and spirituality before departing, the differences were often overwhelming. Here are just a few that we encountered.

- Language. Haitians speak French (as do I, although rusty) and a Creole. A quick way to get off to a bad start is to ask a Haitian in French if they speak French *("Parlez-vous français?")*. The problem is that they'll tend to answer yes *("Oui")* even if they only speak Creole, because there is some shame in not speaking French.
- Ritual. As many as 250-thousand people died in the earthquake – one out of eight people in the Port-au-Prince area. Bodies were taken to mass graves in the

countryside, but nobody knew where. Rituals at the cemetery are considered essential, which left people lost. They would ask me what they should do! The best answer I could give them was to suggest they work with their own spiritual leaders to come up with new ways to grieve. Aim to be sensitive and accepting of varied beliefs and attitudes about death, grief, and rituals. Even within a seemingly similar group, there will be differences. As always, don't judge; reassure people that this is normal.

- Taboo topics. There are at least three topics that Haitians are reluctant to discuss with outsiders: their spiritual beliefs (which have been badly misrepresented in movies, etc.), HIV/AIDS (the nation had the worst outbreak in the world for a period), and child slavery (which remains partially tolerated, sadly). On sensitive topics like these, it is especially important to resist the temptation to probe or judge. On our very last day in the country, a

mother brought her teenage son to our clinic, saying he had experienced "crises" periodically. I'd
heard the Creole/French word "crise" many times
and had been asking follow-up questions to try and
determine if it meant seizures, diabetic issues, or
something else. My translator, with whom I'd
worked for many days, blurted out, "It's *evil,* she
means *evil.*" At that moment, my pre-trip study
paid off because I realized that all of those men-
tions of "crisis" were code for their belief that spirits
sometimes leave bodies, allowing other spirits to
inhabit them. I took it as a compliment that my
translator decided to explain. If he thought I would
judge, I'm sure he would not have.

The hardest hit people are typically those with disabilities. In recent years, this has led to a big effort to address "access and functional needs," or AFN, in disaster response. Be on alert for these. They include health issues, hearing and eyesight limitations, cognitive difficulties, lack of mobility, and the care and safety of service animals. Before disaster hits, it is helpful to learn what organization will lead AFN response, so you know where to send people to obtain things like wheelchairs, walkers, etc.

> Proselytizing – promoting a religion – during an emergency or disaster, is generally discouraged or forbidden by most organizations. As a fire chaplain, I consider it an abuse of my role. If you become aware of such activities, notify leadership or security.

"Do you have religious or spiritual needs?" is an appropriate question. If the answer is yes, ask if they have their own resources they'd like to contact. Otherwise, this is an occasion for referral, ideally to their religious leaders.

Never contradict, correct, or argue with people, even if it seems to you as though their beliefs are contributing to distress. Don't try to answer questions that are rooted in spiritual beliefs or practices. Instead, as always, respond to the emotion behind the words. For example, your response to, "Why did God allow this to happen?" might be "It is hard to make sense of this" or "It is natural to want an explanation and difficult when you don't have one."

Acknowledge survivor's desires to recover religious objects, such as rosaries, statues, or sacred texts. If you can do so safely, you may help them search.

Prayer, alone on in a group, can be comforting. Help people find a suitable place, including identifying the direction in which they might want to face. If invited to join, do not feel obligated, but any genuine gesture of support is helpful. If you are uncertain, ask questions. If you are uncomfortable with survivors' grief practices (they range from quiet to very loud and demonstrative), it is okay to ask for someone else to take over for you. If you are concerned about the effect on other survivors, try and find a more private location.

Death and Grief

As with other kinds of stress, a wide variety of reactions to death or other grief are normal. Anger, sadness, guilt, blame, and the ache of missing them show up frequently. Some people show their grief with tears, others may remain stoic. Reassure them that the different reactions are normal, even if they are wondering why they are not feeling much. You will hear people say that there is no "right way" to grieve. That is true for the same reason you have read here repeatedly – our need to feel some control to moderate stress. The "right" way for people to grieve is for them to be in charge of as much as possible.

I sometimes invite people to say, "My grief is the worst grief because it is *my* grief." That helps prevent "comparison stress shopping." I often include a "ground rule" for this in group settings: "I ask that you not compare how this is for you to how it is for anyone else."

Allowing people to be in charge of their own grief means that there is no timetable or sequence. You may be familiar with Elisabeth Kübler-Ross's "five stages" of grief (which was expanded to seven stages by others). She did not teach that that people go through them sequentially. We bounce around them as the minutes, hours, and days go by (remember – not a straight line, spaghetti). Let people know that even though the feelings come in waves, time can make it easier to live with grief. Notice what that says – *live with* grief. Not "get over" or "move on." Like other high-stress events, losses change our lives forever, so we don't really get over them or move on. No one wants to forget the lost loved one or pretend that their life can be the same again.

As you talk about the one who has died, use their name. Ask the friends and family what they liked to be called and ask permission to call the person by that name. Before referring to a resource you know about, ask them if they have a religious leader, doctor, or someone else who could help them through their grief. If they do not, point them in that direction.

People tend to use a lot of clichés to try and reassure others who are grieving. As you read earlier, avoid them. Clichés are distancing at a time people need closeness. If a statement can be interpreted as "Here is a reason not to feel bad," don't use it and discourage others from it. For example, "She's in a better place," is a meaningful faith statement, but it really is only half of the story. My response, although I would never use it confrontationally, is "Yes, but she's not here and I miss her."

Do not use euphemisms when talking about death. Say the person died, not that they are lost, passed away, gone, or other "easier" words that are too easily misunderstood. This directness is a kindness.

Allow people plenty of time and space to react to receiving news that a loved one is dead. For most people, it won't even feel real for hours, days, or even weeks. Save talking about your reactions for when you are with your own support network. Focus on having empathy and compassion for the people you are there to support.

> People notice what is **not** being said. After a boy was killed biking, his mom wanted to see his body, but no one had said how severe the trauma was. Telling the family was hard, but they had already figured it out from the way everyone was avoiding the subject.

If possible, become familiar with regulations and procedures for death certification, autopsies, and release of remains, so that you can answer questions, or help survivors get answers. Urge people not to deal alone with sights or events that make the death feel more real, such as filling out paperwork and identifying remains.

If you are part of a death notification, realize that you may become a difficult reminder of one of the worst moments of the survivor's lives. Even though at the time they may be grateful and welcoming, they may find it painfully triggering to see or talk to you again. Respect their reaction.

Holidays are tough after a major loss or trauma. Invite people to say, "Not this year" as a simple way to temporarily set aside obligations that feel as though they will take more energy than they give. The reverse is also true: Invite them to embrace rituals or other activities that will give more energy than they take.

Violent death raises the difficult question of whether family will view remains. While you absolutely must respect family member's wishes, you may suggest that it is not desirable to have their final sight of their loved one's body to be painful. Using a photograph in place of viewing the body may be an acceptable substitute. Also know that sometimes funeral homes can do wonders.

After responding to a death, you may find yourself curious about who the deceased was. Reading obituaries, news articles, or looking at the deceased's social media profiles are normal responses. However, never become intrusive. You should only attend a funeral or other service with the family's permission. If you find that this curiosity persists for more than a short time, you would be wise to talk over your reactions with someone supportive. You may discover that something in the situation has personal relevance to you, which you need to express and acknowledge. If you don't feel such curiosity, that's perfectly normal, too.

Children and Families

Your approach with children during disasters and other crises will vary according to their age – preschoolers, elementary school age, and adolescents. All children ideally should not be around extremely distraught or angry people. They get their cues from adults, so the company of calm and organized people will go a long way. If they see upset adults, explain that sometimes it takes people time to calm down after an emergency. Reassure them that the person has, or is going to get, the help they need.

Rather than working directly with preschoolers, help their parents (and all other parents) understand what kind of reactions are normal. Emphasize the children's need for stability and calm. Developmental regression is not unusual and commonly shows up in language, toilet training, or other behavior. Clinging and increased separation anxiety are also typical for little ones.

> Developmental interruptions, delays, and regression are typical responses to crisis. The NCTSN/VA PFA field manual includes a detailed list of milestones by age, which can help you normalize changes for survivors.

Reassure parents that this is normal and temporary. Preschoolers need a predictable, familiar routine established as soon as possible. When a caregiver is missing or gone, a substitute can help by asking children if they are doing things "right" – the way it was done before. It is normal for children to be angry with a new caregiver, especially when they are disciplined.

Older children, who are not yet adolescents, also need to be shielded from disturbing information, sights, and sounds. Turn off the TV news and watch their internet activity. Children in this this age group often process grief and trauma through art and play. Their play may act out the crisis; it may also be more aggressive than usual. Let parents know that although this is normal, the children still need boundaries. Regression and clinging are also normal and not unusual. It is okay for kids this age to sleep in the same bed with parents temporarily after a crisis. Play can also be a way to teach young children – showing them that their toy figures "need" rest, exercise, regular food and water is a way to remind and let them practice taking care of themselves.

During an emergency, you may create a child-friendly, safe space, away from operations. Adults in charge should be experienced with children and may need to be cleared by law enforcement. Have a system for ensuring that children only leave with a parent or authorized caregiver. Older children can be engaged to lead activities.

Treat adolescents the same way you talk to adults – but don't expect them to react like adults! It is okay to give them disturbing information but offer it factually and calmly. Younger adolescents are prone to "filling in the gaps" with rumor and imagination, which can escalate the situation rather than defusing it. Art is often especially powerful for teens. Our team often encourages having butcher paper and coloring supplies for them to make posters for themselves and families of those who are ill or lost. Normal reactions include strong feelings of unfairness and resentment.

Children, like everyone else, can be each other's best support. Group activities, games, and especially shared art projects (which do not have to be explicitly related to the crisis) can be distracting, calming, and healing.

As with others, never give children information you are not certain about, including making them promises about what will happen. If they are separated from their parents or other caregivers, they are likely to be quite upset until they see them.

When someone dies, younger children may compare it to the death of a pet. This can feel like minimizing; reassure others that this is a normal, typical response for kids whose only experience of death has been a pet. If you need to explain death to a young child, something like this works: "She can't talk or play with you any more, but she is not hurting."

The younger children are, the less likely they are to have the vocabulary to describe what they are feeling. You can suggest words, but also realize that play, music, art, or other activities may be what they need more than conversation. You may also ask about how they feel physically, such as, "How do you feel inside?" If they have some vocabulary, it is still good to help them by offering choices for them to pick, but don't suggest extreme words that could increase their distress: "Do you feel sad, or scared, or okay right now?"

Children can also draw themselves and describe what they are feeling using the picture.

With all children, just as with adults, don't pressure them to talk until they are ready. Remember, your job is to make it *safe* to talk, not to probe.

> Parents become more protective after a crisis. Adolescents, already struggling for independence, need to understand that their parents are likely to be stricter and more protective. Acknowledge that this is normal but shouldn't *remain* the norm.

Let adults know that following a death, small children may ask the same questions repeatedly, such as "Where is Grampa?" Those reminders can be painful, but it is important to patiently repeat answers.

Children often will worry that another family member will die. Parents sometimes struggle with making a promise that they will always be there for their children, knowing that any of us can die at any time. You can tell them they can tell their kids that they will always care for someone or that someone will always be there to care for them. They need that reassurance. Children who lose a caregiver also need reassurance that it wasn't what that person wanted. It is also normal for children to wonder if a death was punishment or caused by something they did. If this comes up, reassure them that it was not. (Recall that when we have someone to blame, including ourselves, that produces a sense of control that our stress autopilot craves.)

Excluding children from grief rituals – funerals, burial, and so forth – is nearly always a mistake. Include them in your planning, give them a choice of ways to participate or not, such as who to sit with. That person should be prepared to

accompany the child if they want to leave early. If they don't want to attend, give them a choice about who to stay with during the service. If they don't want to, or feel they cannot, participate, offer to say or read something on their behalf. Adults who were excluded from these activities as children often have regrets or unresolved grief.

You don't have to tell children everything. For example, when my younger sister died, we did not want to have to explain cremation to her five-year-old (if it had become necessary, we would have explained that her mommy couldn't feel anything). We had a memorial service and quietly placed the urn with Lesley's ashes out of sight, so that our family knew it was present. At some point in the following years, as she learned more about death, she asked and learned that her mother was cremated.

> As with everyone else, it is okay to tell children "I don't know." You might want to often add, "It is hard not knowing."

Families recover faster and better when they reestablish their routines – meals, sleep schedules, reading, play, and other shared activities. Let them know that differing reactions over time is normal and can become difficult when it seems as if some have moved on or gotten over the crisis or loss. Help them realize that it is healthy to have good and bad times, but they won't always be in sync, so it is important to be patient with one another. Communication is key, so encourage them to let one another know when they are struggling. Parents need to know that children, especially, may act out grief or trauma with aggressiveness or temper tantrums.

Angry People

California's 2020 wildland fire season was the worst in living memory. A dry lightning storm on August 16th sparked thousands of fires. Hundreds of them grew large and uncontrolled. Although people are generally grateful and welcoming of firefighters, we encountered some who showed us little but anger. More than once, I found myself listening to exhausted, furious residents as they saw their homes and livelihoods burn. We had to prioritize suppression efforts according to the threat to values and the likelihood that we could make a difference. But there was no explaining that to people angered by seeing engines race past their burning property.

Firefighters are action-oriented, problem-solving people, so our instinct is to explain and defend our actions. No one is likely to even hear logic when they are angry. You can help control your own reactions by reminding yourself that they are angry at the disaster. It isn't fair of them to take it out on you, but accepting unfairness is an essential crisis response skill. If you struggle with it, talk to your team leadership or another trusted companion.

When your job is support, the best way to respond to anger is to listen. Quietly, calmly, listen. Without trivializing, acknowledge what you hear. If you can honestly agree with something, say so. For example, during one of our huge fires, a furious resident and volunteer firefighter complained that we weren't asking for locals' advice. Although I wasn't sure that was true, I emphatically agreed that getting local information is vital. I told him that we are trained to learn from locals about roads, weather, and water supplies, which makes us more effective and could save our own lives.

It is hard to listen to intense criticism without become defensive. I remind myself that people are angry about what is happening to their community, their home, their business. Blaming us is a natural response. *Don't take it personally* is good life guidance, which becomes crucial in a crisis.

Help angry people to prioritize. I persuaded one fuming farmer (who had barely slept in days) to prioritize by telling him (after mostly just listening for about 20 minutes!) that I could probably get him five minutes with our Planning Section Chief, the senior person at our fire camp.

"If you could tell him just one thing, what would it be?" I asked. Once he decided what that would be, I grabbed the chief and coached him, "Don't argue, please just listen to him and agree with whatever you can." The conversation went well – the farmer needed to be heard. As we walked out

> Self-control becomes more difficult when we are HALTed – Hungry, Angry, Lonely, or Tired.

of our tent, he said, "I feel much calmer now." I was surprised. Even though I know these methods can be effective, I don't assume they will be. Sometimes they do not; manage your expectations.

If all you do is succeed in resisting the natural urge to explain and defend your own or others' actions, you'll avoid making the situation worse. Keep in mind that when people are highly stressed, logic goes out the window.

Help survivors cope with angry friends or relatives by normalizing it – tell them that there is plenty to be angry about and invite them to also not take it personally, but acknowledge how difficult that can be, especially when their own stress reactions are active.

While acknowledging and normalizing anger like other emotions, remind people that excessive angry becomes an obstacle. Invite them to take some time to cool down, talk to a friend, exercise, or distract themselves for a while. If they are hungry, eat. If tired, rest or sleep. Aim to help them direct their energy toward problem-solving.

When you sense that someone's anger is out of control or poses a threat, get medical or law enforcement help.

Rumors and Conspiracy Theories

Conspiracy theories can offer a sense of control, reducing our threat response, when helplessness feels overwhelming.

For example, if the Covid-19 pandemic came from a random virus mutation, then we had no control over it. But, if it was designed in a laboratory (conspiracy theory), then someone did have control over it. When we feel like somebody has – or could have had – control, our brain's stress autopilot calms down. The appeal of this is not about what we *think,* but about what we *feel.*

Helplessness, lack of control and the inability to do anything about a perceived risk all trigger a *threat* response; a stronger stress reaction than that which applies to ordinary challenges. Conspiracy theories mitigate the stress by making people feel as if we are not – or were not –

helpless. Even when reflecting on the past, if it feels as if somebody *could* have done something to stop the threat, that's reassuring, because our stress autopilot is always planning and rehearsing for future risks, based on past experiences.[5]

"Just Stay Positive"

When my closest friend's toddler suffered and died from a brain tumor, well-meaning people would sometimes say, "Everything happens for a reason." Aside from the pain of hearing a cliché, he found the idea that his child's death was intentional to be offensive. Dave's response was, "Everything happens for a reason, *and sometimes we make it up right afterwards.*"

---

[5] Adapted from *Resilience During the Pandemic.*

In religion, finding the good in a bad event is called "redemption." That is a much more comprehensible and palatable idea than the cliché. Making meaning from horrible events helps, but it cannot be rushed. Never push people to find or make meaning from a terrible event. When Dave looks back to when his son was ill and died, along with the suffering he also remembers how his family was surrounded and supported by friends and communities. He calls it bittersweet, which is surely as good as the memories of losing a child can become.

Recall that under stress, our brains tend toward "binary thinking" – all this or that, nothing in between. Staying in that state of mind gets people stuck in grief. Allowing the positives and negatives to co-exist is healthy. As someone coined, life is "brute-iful" – brutal and beautiful. It includes what I call "horrible privileges," from changing diapers to attending to the death of a loved one.

About the Author

Nick Arnett is a CERT and Critical Incident Stress Management (CISM) leader and instructor, fire chaplain, Firefighter, EMT, Medical Unit Leader, Public Information Officer, and former software founder and executive, journalist, and paramedic with experience in domestic and international disaster response who has led hundreds of crisis intervention and peer support responses for schools, the public and first responder agencies, including as a consultant to California's state fire department and other public safety agencies. He is a member of the California Fire Chaplain Association, the executive board of the California Peer Support Association, and co-chair of Santa Clara County's Collaborating Agencies Disaster Response Effort's pandemic emotional/spiritual response. Arnett received a Volunteer of the Year award from the Santa Clara County Emergency Managers Association in 2012 and a

Crystal Bowl award from the San Jose Junior League, with recognitions from local, state, and federal elected officials.

Resources

- The CERT Disaster Psychology module.
- Social media:
    - ○ @StressIntoStrengthBook on Facebook.
    - ○ @NickArnett on Twitter
    - ○ Stress Into Strength on YouTube
- SAMHSA, the Substance Abuse and Mental Health Administration.
- CrisisResponse.org (training)
- NCTSN/VA Field Manual and Online Training.
- International Critical Incident Stress Foundation.
- The United States Air Force Master Resilience Training curriculum.
- Recommended books on Goodreads:
  http://bit.ly/StressIntoStrengthRecommends